Learning Proxmox VE

Unleash the power of Proxmox VE by setting up a dedicated virtual environment to serve both containers and virtual machines

Rik Goldman

BIRMINGHAM - MUMBAI

Learning Proxmox VE

First published: March 2016

Production reference: 1290316

Published by Packt Publishing Ltd.

Livery Place

35 Livery Street

Birmingham B3 2PB, UK.

ISBN 978-1-78398-178-6

www.packtpub.com

Credits

Author

Rik Goldman

Reviewer

Ludovic L'HOIR

Acquisition Editor

Sonali Vernekar

Content Development Editor

Anish Dhurat

Technical Editor

Ryan Kochery

Copy Editor

Merilyn Pereira

Project Coordinator

Bijal Patel

Proofreader

Safis Editing

Indexer

Mariammal Chettiyar

Graphics

Kirk D'Penha
Disha Haria

Production Coordinator

Arvindkumar Gupta

About the Author

Rik Goldman had 18 years of professional IT experience and 17 years of teaching experience when he became the director of technology and a teacher of advanced computing at Chelsea School in 2012.

Throughout his 10 years at the university, he concentrated on literary computing, new media, humanities computing, and virtuality. At first, Rik supported his studies by developing institutional websites and database applications; eventually, however, he became the administrator of Solaris and Irix servers for West Virginia University's Center for Literary Computing, a lab committed to the study of electronic texts, virtuality, and digital composition and rhetoric.

In the classroom, Rik's commitment to authentic teaching and learning as well as his advocacy of social justice and equity have placed him at the vanguard of technology education. Working with and learning from his students, he has overseen projects that have provided real solutions for school infrastructure, data management, and programming. His many accomplishments reveal an educator who strives to provide authentic opportunities for learning and engagement, but his true legacy lies in what he has engendered in his students: a desire for knowledge, a critical urge, and an analyst's zeal for complex abstractions. Through this work with students and his responsibilities as a systems administrator, Rik has enjoyed a productive preoccupation with virtualization technologies and their impact on popular culture.

Since his full-time adoption of Red Hat 5 at home, he has been committed to GNU/Linux and the underlying philosophies that have made it so successful. Consequently, he is a passionate advocate of open source and free software. Together with his students, he has contributed to the success of a myriad open source endeavors by developing documentation, writing code, and mentoring communities of young developers from around the world.

In his free time, Rik enjoys reading literature, exploring critical theory, listening to records, and traveling to concerts with his family.

Acknowledgments

This book could not have been realized without the kind patience, understanding, and encouragement of Sabre Goldman and our remarkable son, Ender Ripley. Whatever fantastic adventures I dream of, it's through Sabre's unflagging support and enduring patience that those impossible dreams are realized.

The importance that my mother places on the power of words, text, and narrative continues to influence my life's trajectory and always propels me toward opportunities to find the right word. Without her, I wouldn't have had the interest or skills to pursue this opportunity.

Thanks to the Chelsea School community, particularly my colleagues and students, without whom there's no me. I am lucky to be a part of a community that never fails to inspire me to learn, develop, share, and improve.

My sincerest thanks go out to Tim Bielawa, the author of *The Linux Sysadmin's Guide to Virtual Disks*. By posting a public draft of his work in progress, he did this project significant good. Cheers to Tim and so many others who contribute documentation of open source projects.

About the Reviewer

Ludovic L'HOIR is 42 years old and has worked in the IT sector for the past 15 years . He first studied Greek Archeology then after his diploma he decided to change his life and left France to live in Australia for about 2 years. He started his IT career at Reuters SA in 2001 in Geneva as a Network Controller Specialist. In 2005, he founded a company that was the first open source cybercafe in France. His career continued as an IT systems administrator at the IT lab of CNRS. Ludovic also worked at Concorde Logistics (OBS) as a Networks and Systems Manager. After this rich experience, he joined MICHELIN (Tyredating) in September 2010 as CTO. Currently, he is the IT Manager of S4M (Success for Mobile), which is a mobile-native ad tech company transforming ads into genuine personalized content for each individual user.

Ludovic is passionate about childhood development. He enjoys writing books for young children (`http://ludobooks.fr`) and also participating in the doudoulinux project (a Linux distribution especially designed for children to make computer usage as easy and pleasant as possible for them `http://doudoulinux.org`). In his spare time, Ludovic likes cooking food from different cultures. He lives in the South of France with his wife and 9 year old daughter.

www.PacktPub.com

For support files and downloads related to your book, please visit www.PacktPub.com .

eBooks, discount offers, and more

Did you know that Packt offers eBook versions of every book published, with PDF and ePub files available? You can upgrade to the eBook version at www.PacktPub.com and as a print book customer, you are entitled to a discount on the eBook copy. Get in touch with us at customercare@packtpub.com for more details.

At www.PacktPub.com, you can also read a collection of free technical articles, sign up for a range of free newsletters and receive exclusive discounts and offers on Packt books and eBooks.

https://www2.packtpub.com/books/subscription/packtlib

Do you need instant solutions to your IT questions? PacktLib is Packt's online digital book library. Here, you can search, access, and read Packt's entire library of books.

Why subscribe?

- Fully searchable across every book published by Packt
- Copy and paste, print, and bookmark content
- On demand and accessible via a web browser

Free access for Packt account holders

Get notified! Find out when new books are published by following @PacktEnterprise on Twitter or the Packt Enterprise Facebook page.

Table of Contents

Preface

"There is a double spooking the world, the double of abstraction. The fortunes of states and armies, companies and communities depend on it. All contending classes - the landlords and farmers, the workers and capitalists - revere yet fear the relentless abstraction of the world on which their fortunes yet depend. All the classes but one. The hacker class."

"The virtual is the true domain of the hacker. It is from the virtual that the hacker produces ever-new expressions of the actual. To the hacker, what is represented as being real is always partial, limited, perhaps even false. To the hacker there is always a surplus of possibility expressed in what is actual, the surplus of the virtual. This is the inexhaustible domain of what is real without being actual, what is not but which may be. To hack is to release the virtual into the actual, to express the difference of the real."

– McKenzie Wark, A Hacker Manifesto

Not so many years ago, it would've taken three computers to author this book efficiently on the go. Virtualization, however, has made it possible to write without the obscene hassle of dragging about so much baggage. Virtualization has reduced labor and energy expenditure and maximized productivity and discretionary time during the writing and production of this book.

Abstraction liberates us from material constraints, leaving in their place the privilege of nostalgia — tractor-fed edge strips, darkroom chemicals, printing presses and type-set trays, overflowing money bags with dollar signs, and of course, cramped server rooms.

Through server virtualization, the abstraction of computing resources from physical systems has overturned data centers and radically upset the traditional and repetitive routines of system engineers and administrators in favor of efficiency, conservation, lowered expenditure, secure systems, and the simple deployment of automation to complete repetitive tasks.

Proxmox VE has been a pioneering agent in this rapid revolution since the 2008 release of version 1.0 — the first hypervisor to support both virtual machines and containers.

With version 4.2 in the works, and the industry's fascination finally fixed on the realization of a container revolution, Proxmox VE still provides an open source, enterprise virtualization solution with premium support that enjoys tremendous international popularity — even as competing brands have scrambled to roll out container solutions just in time.

This book is packed with introductory concepts and best practice techniques for experienced Linux users eager to take advantage of bleeding edge virtualization strategies and practices with Proxmox VE.

This book explores the benefits of two of these complementary virtualization technologies, containers and virtual machines, so you'll be forearmed to make informed and deliberated choices regarding the best paths for virtualizing your data center.

What this book covers

Chapter 1, *Proxmox VE Fundamentals*, outlines Proxmox VE's features and distinguishing characteristics and briefly compares and contrasts virtual machines and containers.

Chapter 2, *Installing Proxmox VE*, goes through the Proxmox VE installation process after covering Proxmox VE's hardware requirements and discussing minimal and optimal hardware specifications.

Chapter 3, *Creating Containers*, starts with a primer on containers and their uses before providing a walkthrough of the container creation processes, including choosing and downloading an OS or virtual appliance template.

Chapter 4, *Creating Virtual Machines*, first elaborates on the functional differences between virtual machines and suggests prospective use cases and the inherent benefits and drawbacks of full virtualization. It then walks through the process of creating and configuring virtual machines intended for Microsoft Windows Server and Fedora Server.

Chapter 5, *Working with Virtual Disks*, compares and contrasts virtual hard disk options, including disk image types, virtual bus/interfaces, and cache types.

Chapter 6, *Networking with Proxmox VE*, contrasts common virtual Ethernet adaptor options provided by Proxmox VE and works to articulate use cases for each.

Chapter 7, *Securing Proxmox VE*, enumerates strategies for mitigating security threats to virtualized datacenters in general, and Proxmox VE hosts and guests in particular.

What you need for this book

Working with the illustrative examples in this book will require a 64-bit machine to host Proxmox 4.1 that meets at least the minimum recommended specs for evaluation:

- CPU: 64 bit (Intel EMT64 or AMD64)
- Intel VT/AMD-V capable CPU/Mainboard (for KVM Full Virtualization support)
- A minimum of 1 GB RAM
- Hard drive
- One NIC compatible with RedHat Enterprise Linux

This is not an ideal rig—more powerful specs can be found in Chapter 2, *Installing Proxmox VE*.

In addition to a machine to host Proxmox VE, broadband internet access is assumed, as is a remote workstation on the same LAN as the Proxmox VE host, a modern, JavaScript-enabled web browser, and installed ssh and sftp clients.

Who this book is for

This book is intended for server and system administrators and engineers who are eager to take advantage of the potential of virtual machines and containers to manage servers more efficiently and make the best use of resources, from energy consumption to hardware utilization to physical real estate.

Conventions

In this book, you will find a number of text styles that distinguish between different kinds of information. Here are some examples of these styles and an explanation of their meaning.

Code words in text, database table names, folder names, filenames, file extensions, pathnames, dummy URLs, user input, and Twitter handles are shown as follows: "We can use the qm create command to create a Proxmox VE virtual machine."

Any command-line input or output is written as follows:

```
-ostype win8 \
-sockets 1
```

New terms and **important words** are shown in bold. Words that you see on the screen, for example, in menus or dialog boxes, appear in the text like this: "Proceed with the installation by pressing *i* or navigating to **Install Fedora 23**."

Warnings or important notes appear in a box like this.

Tips and tricks appear like this.

Reader feedback

Feedback from our readers is always welcome. Let us know what you think about this book—what you liked or disliked. Reader feedback is important for us as it helps us develop titles that you will really get the most out of.

To send us general feedback, simply e-mail feedback@packtpub.com, and mention the book's title in the subject of your message.

If there is a topic that you have expertise in and you are interested in either writing or contributing to a book, see our author guide at www.packtpub.com/authors.

Customer support

Now that you are the proud owner of a Packt book, we have a number of things to help you to get the most from your purchase.

Downloading the example code

You can download the example code files for this book from your account at http://www.packtpub.com. If you purchased this book elsewhere, you can visit http://www.packtpub.com/support and register to have the files e-mailed directly to you.

You can download the code files by following these steps:

1. Log in or register to our website using your e-mail address and password.
2. Hover the mouse pointer on the **SUPPORT** tab at the top.
3. Click on **Code Downloads & Errata**.
4. Enter the name of the book in the **Search** box.
5. Select the book for which you're looking to download the code files.
6. Choose from the drop-down menu where you purchased this book from.
7. Click on **Code Download**.

Once the file is downloaded, please make sure that you unzip or extract the folder using the latest version of:

- WinRAR / 7-Zip for Windows
- Zipeg / iZip / UnRarX for Mac
- 7-Zip / PeaZip for Linux

Downloading the color images of this book

We also provide you with a PDF file that has color images of the screenshots/diagrams used in this book. The color images will help you better understand the changes in the output. You can download this file from `http://www.packtpub.com/sites/default/files/downloads/LearningProxmoxVE_ColorImages.pdf`.

Errata

Although we have taken every care to ensure the accuracy of our content, mistakes do happen. If you find a mistake in one of our books—maybe a mistake in the text or the code—we would be grateful if you could report this to us. By doing so, you can save other readers from frustration and help us improve subsequent versions of this book. If you find any errata, please report them by visiting `http://www.packtpub.com/submit-errata`, selecting your book, clicking on the **Errata Submission Form** link, and entering the details of your errata. Once your errata are verified, your submission will be accepted and the errata will be uploaded to our website or added to any list of existing errata under the Errata section of that title.

To view the previously submitted errata, go to https://www.packtpub.com/books/content/support and enter the name of the book in the search field. The required information will appear under the Errata section.

Piracy

Piracy of copyrighted material on the Internet is an ongoing problem across all media. At Packt, we take the protection of our copyright and licenses very seriously. If you come across any illegal copies of our works in any form on the Internet, please provide us with the location address or website name immediately so that we can pursue a remedy.

Please contact us at copyright@packtpub.com with a link to the suspected pirated material.

We appreciate your help in protecting our authors and our ability to bring you valuable content.

Questions

If you have a problem with any aspect of this book, you can contact us at questions@packtpub.com, and we will do our best to address the problem.

1
Proxmox VE Fundamentals

Proxmox Virtual Environment (**PVE**) is a mature, complete, well-supported, enterprise-class virtualization environment for servers. It is an open source tool — based in the Debian GNU/Linux distribution — that manages containers, virtual machines, storage, virtualized networks, and high-availability clustering through a well-designed, web-based interface or via the command-line interface.

 Developers provided the first stable release of Proxmox VE in 2008; four years and eight point releases later, ZDNet's Ken Hess boldly, but quite sensibly, declared Proxmox VE as *Proxmox: The Ultimate Hypervisor* (`http://www.zdnet.com/article/proxmox-the-ultimate-hypervisor/`). Four years later, PVE is on version 4.1, in use by at least 90,000 hosts, and more than 500 commercial customers in 140 countries; the web-based administrative interface itself is translated into 19 languages.

This chapter explores the fundamental technologies underlying PVE's hypervisor features: **LXC**, **KVM**, and **QEMU**. To do so, we will develop a working understanding of virtual machines, containers, and their appropriate use.

We will cover the following topics in this chapter:

- Proxmox VE in brief
- Virtualization and containerization with PVE
- Proxmox VE virtual machines, KVM, and QEMU
- Containerization with PVE and LXC

Proxmox VE in brief

With Proxmox VE, Proxmox Server Solutions GmbH (`https://www.proxmox.com/en/about`) provides us with an enterprise-ready, open source *type* 2 *Hypervisor*. Later, you'll find some of the features that make Proxmox VE such a strong enterprise candidate.

- The license for Proxmox VE is very deliberately the *GNU Affero General Public License (V3)* (`https://www.gnu.org/licenses/agpl-3.0.html`). From among the many free and open source compatible licenses available, this is a significant choice because it is "specifically designed to ensure cooperation with the community in the case of network server software."
- PVE is primarily administered from an integrated web interface, from the command line locally, or via SSH. Consequently, there is no need for a separate management server and the associated expenditure. In this way, Proxmox VE significantly contrasts with alternative enterprise virtualization solutions by vendors such as VMware.
- Proxmox VE instances/nodes can be incorporated into PVE clusters, and centrally administered from a unified web interface.
- Proxmox VE provides for live migration—the movement of a virtual machine or container from one cluster node to another without any disruption of services. This is a rather unique feature of PVE and not common in competing products.

Features	Proxmox VE	VMware vSphere
Hardware requirements	Flexible	Strict compliance with HCL
Integrated management interface	Web- and shell-based (browser and SSH)	No. Requires dedicated management server at additional cost
Simple subscription structure	Yes; based on number of premium support tickets per year and CPU socket count	No
High availability	Yes	Yes
VM live migration	Yes	Yes
Supports containers	Yes	No
Virtual machine OS support	Windows and Linux	Windows, Linux, and Unix
Community support	Yes	No
Live VM snapshots	Yes	Yes

Contrasting Proxmox VE and VMware vSphere features

For a complete catalog of features, see the Proxmox VE datasheet at `https://www.proxmox.com/images/download/pve/docs/Proxmox-VE-Datasheet.pdf`.

Like its competitors, PVE is a hypervisor: a typical hypervisor is software that creates, runs, configures, and manages virtual machines based on an administrator or engineer's choices.

PVE is known as a type 2 hypervisor because the virtualization layer is built upon an operating system.

As a type 2 hypervisor, Proxmox VE is built on the Debian project. Debian is a GNU/Linux distribution renowned for its reliability, commitment to security, and its thriving and dedicated community of contributing developers.

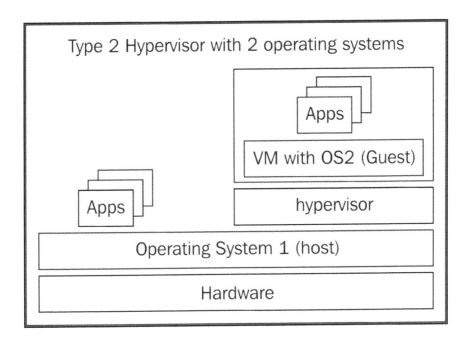

A type 2 hypervisor, such as PVE, runs directly over the operating system. In Proxmox VE's case, the operating system is Debian; since the release of PVE 4.0, the underlying operating system has been Debian "Jessie."

By contrast, a Type I Hypervisor (such as VMware's ESXi) runs directly on bare metal without the mediation of an operating system. It has no additional function beyond managing virtualization and the physical hardware.

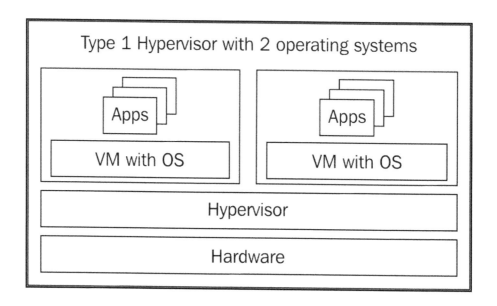

A type I hypervisor runs directly on hardware, without the mediation of an operating system.

Debian-based GNU/Linux distributions are arguably the most popular GNU/Linux distributions for the desktop.

One characteristic that distinguishes Debian from competing distributions is its release policy: Debian releases only when its development community can ensure its *stability*, *security*, and *usability*.

Debian does not distinguish between long-term support releases and regular releases as do some other distributions.

Instead, all Debian releases receive strong support and critical updates throughout the first year following the next release. (Since 2007, a major release of Debian has been made about every two years. Debian 8, *Jessie*, was released just about on schedule in 2015.

Proxmox VE's reliance on Debian is thus a testament to its commitment to these values: stability, security, and usability during scheduled releases that favor cutting-edge features.

PVE provides its virtualization functionality through three open technologies managed through a unified web-based interface:

- LXC
- KVM
- QEMU

To understand how this foundation serves Proxmox VE, we must first be able to clearly understand the relationship between virtualization (or, specifically, *hardware virtualization*) and containerization (*OS virtualization*). As we proceed, their respective use cases should become clear.

Virtualization with Proxmox VE

It is correct to ultimately understand containerization as a type of virtualization. However, here, we'll look first to conceptually distinguish a virtual machine from a container by focusing on contrasting characteristics.

Simply put, virtualization is a technique through which we provide fully-functional, computing resources without a demand for the resources' physical organization, locations, or relative proximity.

Virtualization technology allows us to share and allocate the resources of a physical computer with multiple execution environments. Without context, virtualization is a vague term. It encapsulates the abstraction of such resources as storage, networks, servers, desktop environments, and even applications from their concrete hardware requirements through software implementation solutions called **hypervisors**.

Virtualization thus affords us more flexibility, more functionality, and a significant positive impact on our budgets which are often realized with merely the resources we have at hand.

In terms of PVE, virtualization most commonly refers to the abstraction of all aspects of a discrete computing system from its hardware. In this context, virtualization is the creation, in other words, of a virtual machine or VM, with its own operating system and applications.

A VM may be initially understood as a computer that has the same functionality as a physical machine. Likewise, it may be incorporated and communicated with via a network exactly as a machine with physical hardware would. Put yet another way, from inside a VM, we will experience no difference from which we can distinguish it from a physical computer.

The virtual machine, moreover, hasn't the physical footprint of its physical counterparts. The hardware it relies on is, in fact, provided by software that borrows from the hardware resources of a host installed on a physical machine (or **bare metal**).

Nevertheless, the software components of the virtual machine, from the applications to the operating system, are distinctly separated from those of the host machine. This advantage is realized when it comes to allocating physical space for resources.

For example, we may have a PVE server running a web server, database server, firewall, and log management system—all as discrete virtual machines. Rather than consuming physical space, resources, and labor of maintaining four physical machines, we simply make physical room for the single Proxmox VE server and configure an appropriate virtual LAN as necessary.

In a white paper entitled *Putting Server Virtualization to Work*, AMD articulates well the benefits of virtualization to businesses and developers (`https://www.amd.com/Document s/32951B_Virtual_WP.pdf`):

Top 5 business benefits of virtualization:

Increases server utilization

Improves service levels

Streamlines manageability and security

Decreases hardware costs

Reduces facility costs

The benefits of virtualization with a development and test environment:

Lowers capital and space requirements

Lowers power and cooling costs

Increases efficiencies through shorter test cycles

Faster time-to-market

To these benefits, let's add portability and encapsulation: the unique ability to migrate a live VM from one PVE host to another—without suffering a service outage.

Proxmox VE makes the creation and control of virtual machines possible through the combined use of two free and open source technologies: **Kernel-based Virtual Machine** (or **KVM**) and (**Quick Emulator (QEMU)**). Used together, we refer to this integration of tools as **KVM-QEMU**.

KVM

KVM has been an integral part of the Linux kernel since February 2007. This kernel module allows GNU/Linux users and administrators to take advantage of an architecture's hardware virtualization extensions; for our purposes, these extensions are AMD's **AMD-V** and Intel's**VT-X** for the x86_64 architecture.

To really make the most of Proxmox VE's feature set, you'll therefore want to install on an x86_64 machine with a CPU that has integrated virtualization extensions. For a full list of AMD and Intel processors supported by KVM, visit Intel at `http://ark.intel.com/Prod ucts/VirtualizationTechnology` or AMD at `http://support.amd.com/en-us/kb-a rticles/Pages/GPU120AMDRVICPUsHyperVWin8.aspx`.

QEMU

QEMU provides an emulation and virtualization interface that can be scripted or otherwise controlled by a user.

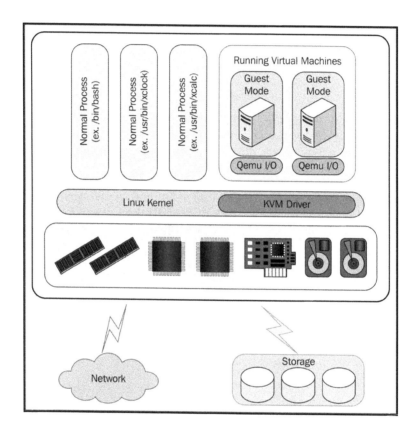

Visualizing the relationship between KVM and QEMU

Without Proxmox VE, we could essentially define the hardware, create a virtual disk, and start and stop a virtualized server from the command line using QEMU.

Alternatively, we could rely on any one of an array of GUI frontends for QEMU (a list of GUIs available for various platforms can be found at `http://wiki.qemu.org/Links#GUI _Front_Ends`).

Of course, working with these solutions is productive only if you're interested in what goes on behind the scenes in PVE when virtual machines are defined. Proxmox VE's management of virtual machines, is itself, managing QEMU through its API.

Managing QEMU from the command line can be tedious. The following is a line from a script that launched Raspbian, a Debian remix intended for the architecture of the Raspberry Pi, on an x86 Intel machine running Ubuntu. When we see how easy it is to manage VMs from Proxmox VE's administrative interfaces, we'll sincerely appreciate that relative simplicity:

```
qemu-system-arm -kernel kernel-qemu -cpu arm1176 -m 256 -
M versatilepb -no-reboot -serial stdio -append
"root=/dev/sda2 panic=1" -hda ./$raspbian_img -hdb swap
```

If you're familiar with QEMU's emulation features, it's perhaps important to note that we can't manage *emulation* through the tools and features Proxmox VE provides—despite its reliance on QEMU. From a bash shell provided by Debian, it's possible. However, the emulation can't be controlled through PVE's administration and management interfaces.

OS Virtualization with Proxmox VE

Containers are another type of virtualization. Synonymous with *OS virtualization*, containers have enjoyed a recent renaissance. In contrast to VMs, containers share operating system components, such as libraries and binaries, with the host operating system; a virtual machine does not.

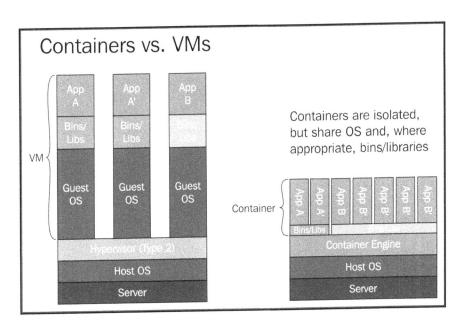

Visually contrasting virtual machines with containers

The container advantage

This arrangement potentially allows a container to run leaner and with fewer hardware resources borrowed from the host. For many authors, pundits, and users, containers also offer a demonstrable advantage in terms of speed and efficiency. (However, it should be noted here that as resources such as RAM and more powerful CPUs become cheaper, this advantage will diminish.)

The Proxmox VE container is made possible through LXC from version 4.0 onwards (it's made possible through OpenVZ in previous PVE versions). LXC is the third fundamental technology serving Proxmox VE's ultimate interest. Like KVM and QEMU, LXC (or Linux Containers) is an open source technology. It allows a host to run, and an administrator to manage, multiple operating system instances as isolated containers on a single physical host. Conceptually then, a container very clearly represents a class of virtualization, rather than an opposing concept. Nevertheless, it's helpful to maintain a clear distinction between a virtual machine and a container as we come to terms with PVE.

The ideal implementation of a Proxmox VE guest is contingent on our distinguishing and choosing between a virtual machine solution and a container solution.

Since Proxmox VE containers share components with the host operating system which offers advantages in terms of efficiency, this text will guide you through the creation of containers whenever the intended guest can be fully realized with Debian *Jessie* as our hypervisor's operating system without sacrificing features.

When our intent is a guest running a Microsoft Windows operating system, for example, a Proxmox VE container ceases to be a solution. In such a case, we turn, instead, to creating a virtual machine. We must rely on a VM precisely because the operating system components that Debian can share with a Linux container are not components that a Microsoft Windows operating system can make use of.

Summary

In this chapter, we have come to terms with the three open source technologies that provide Proxmox VE's foundational features: containerization and virtualization with LXC, KVM, and QEMU.

Along the way, we've come to understand that containers, while being a type of virtualization, have characteristics that distinguish them from virtual machines.

These differences will be crucial as we determine which technology to rely on for a virtual server solution with Proxmox VE.

The next chapter will guide you through the installation and configuration of your first Proxmox VE server. It will thus introduce Proxmox VE hardware specifications and installation methods. Finally, it will provide a thorough walkthrough of the Proxmox Installer.

Let's move forward and prepare our first PVE instance, which we will use to host both containers and virtual machines.

2
Installing Proxmox VE

This chapter is a guide to the installation of Proxmox VE on a physical machine. After completing this chapter, you will have a working PVE server for exploration, experimentation, and perhaps production, depending on your hardware configuration.

Along the way, the chapter will explain how to determine whether a computer's hardware satisfies PVE's minimal or optimal requirements. This chapter also helps us determine whether our configurations make the most of Intel or AMD's virtualization technologies. Finally, it will outline what to expect from the **Proxmox Installer**, and how to initiate and, ultimately, complete the installation and configuration of a new Proxmox VE system.

The chapter is organized sequentially, moving from installation preparations through booting the new server:

- Hardware requirements and recommendations for Proxmox VE
- Downloading Proxmox VE
- Ensuring hardware virtualization (or nested virtualization) is enabled
- Preparing for the Proxmox VE Installer
- Completing the Proxmox VE Installer

 The term **bare metal**, briefly introduced in the previous chapter, refers to a physical computer system that does not have an operating system or any other software installed.

Hardware requirements and recommendations for Proxmox VE

Before starting installation activity, be sure your hardware at least meets PVE's minimum hardware requirements.

The official wiki provides recommended specifications for both evaluation and production scenarios (`https://www.proxmox.com/en/proxmox-ve/requirements`).

However, the *For evaluation* specifications are a bit vague and quite restrictive; they are intended for testing only. You'll find that following them will provide what one needs to become familiar with the installation process and the web-based administration interface. You may even try to run a single, minimal virtual machine and container. *If your goals and objectives are more substantive, however, you're very likely to become frustrated very quickly with these specs.*

The following is the configuration recommended by the Proxmox VE wiki page (`https://pve.proxmox.com/wiki/Installation#Minimum_requirements.2C_for_evaluatio n`) for very basic testing of PVE (release 4.1):

Component	Recommendation
CPU	64-bit (Intel EMT64 or AMD64)
Motherboard	Intel VT/AMD-V capable CPU/Mainboard (for KVM Full Virtualization support)
Memory	Minimum 1 GB RAM
Storage	1 hard disk drive
Network Interface	A single NIC

This vague, minimal suggestion is ideal for someone who's simply learning how to navigate PVE's web-based administration interface; perhaps it's enough to go through the motion of creating a virtual machine or an LXC container. Although the specs are vague, they offer just enough insight to suggest that a machine based on them will not have the resources to support learning the content offered in this text.

On the other hand, if you're fully intending to virtualize your datacenter with PVE, certainly use wiki's specs for a production server as a baseline; a couple of machines built around these specifications provide the resources to not only follow along with this text, but also to practice configuring a high-availability cluster. When you're comfortable with PVE, they'll be waiting to be put to use in production.

For production hardware, the PVE wiki recommends at least a dual- or quad-socket server (`https://pve.proxmox.com/wiki/Installation#Recommended_system_requirements`):

Component	Recommendation
CPU	64-bit Intel EMT64 or AMD64.
Motherboard	Intel VT/AMD-V capable CPU/Mainboard (for KVM Full Virtualization support).
Storage	Hardware RAID with battery-protected write cache (BBU) or flash protection (software RAID is not supported). Fast hard drives: 15k rpm SAS, Raid10 for best results.
RAM	8 GB RAM is good, more is better (increase as much as possible).
Network Interface Cards	Two Gigabit NICs (for bonding)—add additional NICs depending on your preferred storage technology and cluster setup.
Additional Needs	Fencing hardware (only needed for high availability).

If you want to fully engage with this text, which stops short of establishing a high availability system or joining PVE nodes to create a cluster, consider a build such as the following: a simple Intel, single hexa-core or octo-core CPU configuration, a motherboard that supports Intel's virtualization extensions, and a single 1 TB hard disk drive (we'll be consequently restricted to EXT3 or EXT4 filesystems). In addition, you'll want at least 8 GB RAM and a Red Hat Enterprise Linux-compatible network interface card.

The following table offers a wish list of parts with which to build a machine that could be ideal not only for learning Proxmox VE, but also putting it to work in a small enterprise:

Component	Description
CPU	Intel Xeon E5-2620 v3 Hexa-core (6 Core) 2.40 GHz Processor, Socket FCLGA2011 (learn more about this processor at `http://ark.intel.com/products/83352/Intel-Xeon-Processor-E5-2620-v3-15M-Cache-2_40-GHz`).
Motherboard	Supermicro ATX DDR4 LGA 2011 Motherboards X10SRL-F-O (see specifications at `http://www.supermicro.com/products/motherboard/xeon/c600/x10srl-f.cfm`). For more processing power, consider Supermicro's ATX X10DAL-I, which supports two Xeon CPUs (`http://www.supermicro.com/products/motherboard/Xeon/C600/X10DAL-i.cfm`).
RAM	Crucial 32 GB DDR4-2133 LRDIMM (CT6228561). (Learn more about this product at `http://www.crucial.com/usa/en/x10srl-f/CT6228561`.)
Storage	1 TB Western Digital VelociRaptor WD1000DHTZ (`http://www.wdc.com/wdproducts/library/SpecSheet/ENG/2879-701284.pdf`).

The do-it-yourself compromise described offers enough RAM and CPU power to host many virtual servers, both VMs and containers simultaneously, and is thus satisfactory for the tasks in chapters to come.

Alternatively, look to manufacturers such as Lenovo or Dell. Dell, for example, has at least three server-grade machines that are fully customizable starting points. Listed in order of increasing power and versatility, the following rack-mountable servers are highly flexible and very near ideal solutions. Lenovo has comparable products:

- PowerEdge R330 Server (`http://www.dell.com/us/business/p/poweredge-r330/pd#TechSpec`)
- Poweredge R430 Server (`http://www.dell.com/us/business/p/poweredge-r430/pd#TechSpec`)
- PowerEdge R730 Server (`http://www.dell.com/us/business/p/poweredge-r730/pd#TechSpec`)

Once a host system is in hand, downloading the Proxmox VE image in an ISO format is our first step towards a functional server.

Downloading Proxmox VE

An image of the most recent PVE release, 4.1, is available on the Internet via torrent or direct download. The complete ISO is just under 720 MB, and should ultimately be burned to a blank CD or DVD.

Follow these steps to download the torrent file:

1. Navigate to `https://www.proxmox.com/en/downloads/category/iso-images-pve` in your browser.
2. Look for the **Proxmox VE 4.1 ISO Installer (BitTorrent)** subheading.
3. Click on the gray **Download** button to start the download process.

Torrent download

To download directly, use your browser to navigate to the same page, `https://www.proxmox.com/en/downloads/category/iso-images-pve`, and look for the **Proxmox VE 4.1 ISO Installer** subheading. Click on the grey **Download** button to start the download.

Direct download

Note that if you're on an OS X or GNU/Linux workstation, you may choose, of course, to download the disk image from the command line with the `wget` (or `curl`) command. The following line—entered at the terminal—downloads the most recent Proxmox VE release on OS X and GNU/Linux systems to the system's `/tmp` directory. (Details correct as of December 2015; adjust the filename as necessary):

```
wget
http://download.proxmox.com/iso/proxmox-ve_4.1-2f9650d4-2
1.iso -O /tmp/proxmox-ve_4.1-2f9650d4-21.iso
```

Verifying the downloaded image

In the interest of security and your own sanity, be sure to check the `md5sum` value of the downloaded PVE image to make sure it matches the value at `http://download.proxmox.com/iso/MD5SUMS`. In the case of Proxmox VE 4.1, for example, the `md5sum` value is `00358ebcfeea1e33977e1be0fa2e02d3`.

For Ubuntu users, for instance, the following process can be used to verify that the downloaded PVE 4.1 image is as it should be.

Enter the following line in a terminal emulator:

```
md5sum /tmp/proxmox-ve_4.1-2f9650d4-21.iso
```

The response should be as follows:

```
00358ebcfeea1e33977e1be0fa2e02d3  /tmp/proxmox-ve_4.1-2f9650d4-21.iso
```

This response verifies that the `md5sum` value corresponds to the string value provided at `http://download.proxmox.com/iso/MD5SUMS`.

Finally, write the ISO to a blank CD or a USB drive when the download is complete and the `md5sum` value is verified.

 Steps to create a Proxmox VE bootable USB drive, after you have the ISO downloaded, are available at the Proxmox documentation at `https://pve.proxmox.com/wiki/Install_from_USB_Stick`.

Ensuring hardware virtualization extensions are installed

Next, you'll want to ensure that hardware virtualization extensions are enabled on the intended Proxmox VE host.

Assuming there's no operating system on the machine, it's very simple to check this with a Ubuntu Desktop LiveCD. Follow these steps:

1. Download the Ubuntu LiveCD image from `http://www.ubuntu.com/download/desktop` and burn it to a DVD.
2. Boot the new machine from the Ubuntu LiveCD. (For more information on this process, visit `https://help.ubuntu.com/community/LiveCD#How-To_LiveCD_Ubuntu`.)
3. Once the desktop is fully available, open the terminal emulator.
4. For an Intel-based system, enter the following command in the terminal emulator: `egrep -c '(vmx|svm)' /proc/cpuinfo`.

If hardware virtualization extensions are enabled, as is the hope, this command should simply return an integer equal to the number of CPU cores in the machine. If the command returns a 0, hardware virtualization extensions must be enabled in the Intel system's EFI/BIOS.

If your target system is built on the AMD technology, use the following command for a similar effect: `egrep -c ' lm ' /proc/cpuinfo`. Just as described previously, if the command returns a 0, virtualization extensions are not enabled yet. Hopefully, though, the command returns an integer equal to the CPU core count on the system; in this case, your machine is appropriately configured to make use of hardware virtualization technology.

Enabling hardware virtualization extensions

If you discover hardware virtualization extensions are not enabled on your system, they must be enabled in EFI/BIOS.

If you're working with newer hardware, see that the **Virtualization Technology** option in EFI is enabled; in most cases, you'll find this setting under **Advanced CPU Configuration**.

Enabling hardware virtualization technology in EFI/BIOS

On a machine without EFI, you'll likely find the appropriate setting, **Virtualization Technology**, under **Advanced BIOS Features** in the CMOS setup utility.

Preparing for the Proxmox VE Installer

With virtualization extensions enabled and the installation media in hand, it is wise to prepare information the Proxmox Installer will want from you. Having the following information prepared before the Proxmox Installer gets started will help ensure that your configuration is completed with all the consideration and deliberation it deserves.

Have well-considered responses prepared for when you're prompted for the following information by the installer:

- The target installation drive (any existing data on the drive will be permanently deleted)
- The password for the root user
- The administrator's e-mail address
- The country
- The time zone (expressed in this format: Region/City (Pacific/Honolulu, for example)
- The keyboard layout (based on region)
- Whether to use an EXT3 or an EXT4 filesystem (or if you've configured a machine with a RAID10 array, choose `zfs`)
- A fully qualified domain name for the new server
- The fixed IP address to be assigned to the Proxmox VE system
- The IP address of the Internet gateway
- The subnet mask for the network
- The IP address of the DNS server you intend to use (one only)

Regionalization setting such as *time zone* and *keyboard layout* won't affect the language in which Proxmox VE's web-based administration interface communicates.

However, when logging in to the web interface of Proxmox VE 4.1, you'll have the opportunity to choose from among nineteen languages, including, for example, Farsi, Basque, and the two official forms of Norwegian: Bokmål and Nynorsk (`https://www.proxmox.com/en/news/press-releases/proxmox-ve-3-4-released`).

For the command-line interface, you may choose from among the languages available in Debian. Clear steps for identifying the currently selected language and then changing it are provided by the Debian wiki at `https://wiki.debian.org/ChangeLanguage`.

Installing Proxmox VE

The Proxmox Installer takes us through the fundamental configuration details (much as Debian installer does), including the target install drive, locale and keyboard layout, root user credentials, and network configuration.

As the installer walks us through entering these details, it offers impressively clear and concise explanations of what it's asking for and why.

 A video of the full installation process, provided by the developers, is available on YouTube at `https://www.youtube.com/watch?v=ckvPt1 Bp9p0` (do note, however, that it was uploaded in 2011, when Proxmox VE relied on Debian 6).

1. To initiate the installation process, insert and boot from the Proxmox VE installation media.

   To boot from the CD or USB flash drive you've prepared, power on the machine and watch closely for the first screen to appear. Most computers will display, however briefly, some variation of "Press *F12* to choose a Boot Device" toward the bottom of the screen. Quickly press the specified key or combination of keys.

    After a few moments, the monitor should display a menu with a list of boot device candidates. If you burned the Proxmox VE image to CD or DVD, instruct the machine to boot from the optical drive. Otherwise, choose to boot from the USB flash drive you created from the ISO.

   If your machine isn't clear regarding how to change boot options, consult the computer or motherboard manufacturer's documentation. For additional support getting started, see *Before Installing Debain GNU/Linux* at `https://www.debian.org/releases/stable/i386/ch03s06.html .en`.

   After a few moments, the installer should start (as shown in the following screenshot).

Select **Install Proxmox VE** to start the installer.

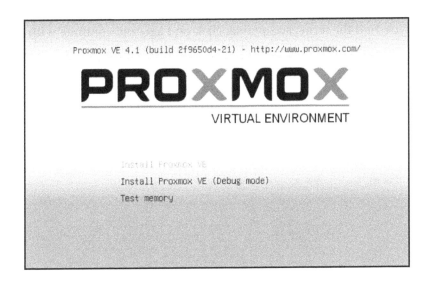

2. The computer will now boot from the install media.

```
[    1.991849] Section-unaligned hotplug range: start 0x10000000, size 0x3400000
0
[    1.991853] acpi PNP0C80:02: add_memory failed
[    1.991854] acpi PNP0C80:02: acpi_memory_enable_device() error
Proxmox startup
mounting proc filesystem
mounting sys filesystem
comandline: BOOT_IMAGE=/boot/linux26 ro ramdisk_size=16777216 rw quiet splash=silent
loading drivers:  shpchp i2c_piix4 pata_acpi mptspi 8250_fintek floppy mac_hid input_leds serio_raw psmouse pcspkr aesni_intel g
hash_clmulni_intel crc32_pclmul crct10dif_pclmul kvm_intel intel_powerclamp x86_pkg_temp_thermal intel_rapl
[    4.052395] piix4_smbus 0000:00:07.3: SMBus Host Controller not enabled!
[    4.405112] sd 2:0:0:0: [sda] Assuming drive cache: write through
modprobe: ERROR: could not insert 'ghash_clmulni_intel': Invalid argument
modprobe: ERROR: could not insert 'intel_powerclamp': No such device
modprobe: ERROR: could not insert 'x86_pkg_temp_thermal': No such device
[    4.518488] intel_rapl: no valid rapl domains found in package 0
modprobe: ERROR: could not insert 'intel_rapl': No such device
searching for cdrom
testing cdrom /dev/sr0
found proxmox cdrom
Starting Proxmox installation
Installing additional hardware drivers
[ ok ] Starting the hotplug events dispatcher: udevd.
[ ok ] Synthesizing the initial hotplug events...done.
[....] Waiting for /dev to be fully populated...[    5.364469] Error: Driver 'pcspkr' is already registered, aborting...
[    5.806894] intel_rapl: no valid rapl domains found in package 0
[    5.826773] intel_rapl: no valid rapl domains found in package 0
done.
Detecting network settings... _
```

Booting to the PVE installer

The machine will soon boot into a mouse-driven graphical user environment as it begins to collect information. Before the installer really does its job, it asks you to agree to the terms of an **end-user license agreement** (**EULA**). If you find the terms acceptable, click on **I agree** to continue with the installation process.

Agreeing to the EULA

3. In the next dialog, you're prompted to choose a target drive for the installation. In addition, this dialog provides an **Options** button that offers an opportunity to choose the filesystem that best suits your needs. As pictured in the following screenshot, if you have a single drive, you're limited in your choice to **ext3**, **ext4**, or **xfs**. Otherwise, you're expected to take advantage of **zfs** and specify a RAID configuration:

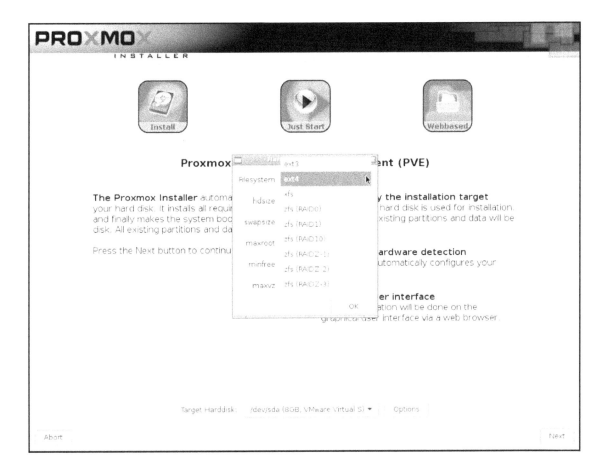

Targeting a storage device and choosing a filesystem

Click on **Next** to move to the next dialog: configuring the system's locale.

4. The next step, illustrated in the following screenshot, is to configure your **Country**, **Time zone**, and **Keyboard Layout**.

Configuring Locale with Proxmox VE Installer

Click on **Next** to finalize the locale.

5. Use the next dialog to set and confirm the password for the new system's root user.

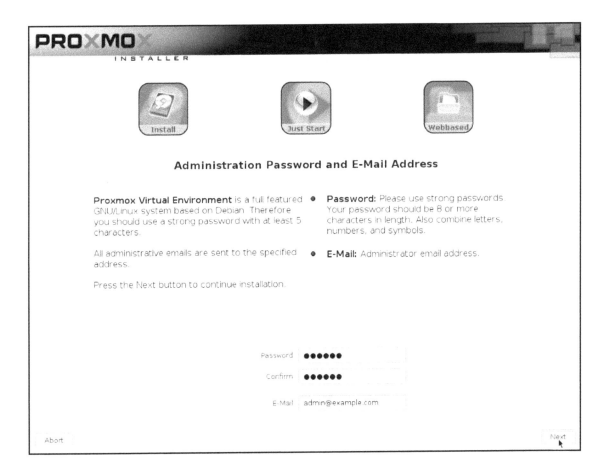

Set the administrator's e-mail and click on **Next** to move forward with the installation and configuration process.

6. Next, configure networking by entering the **Hostname (FQDN)** (fully-qualified domain name), **IP Address**, **DNS Server**, **Netmask**, and **Gateway**, as follows:

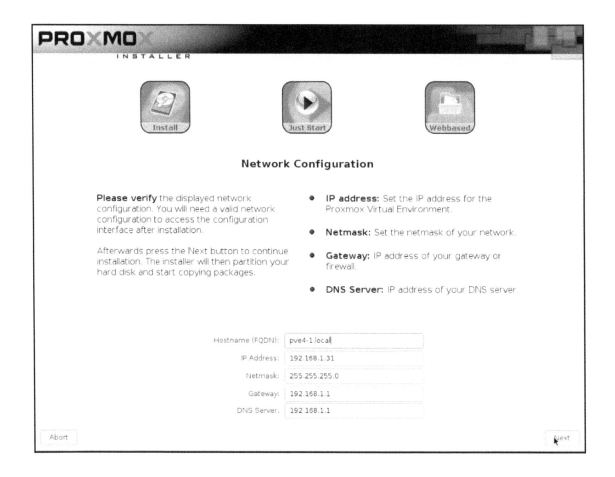

Initial network configuration

When you're satisfied with the network configuration, click on **Next** to commit the configuration and allow the installer to proceed.

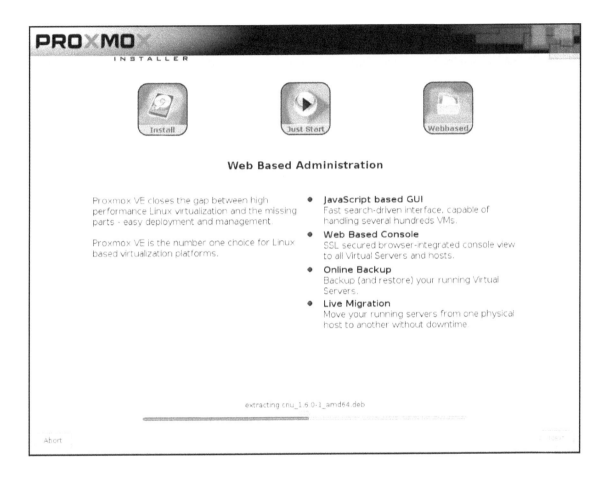

PVE installation at the half-way point

After a confirmation prompt, the installation begins. It can take several minutes to complete; in the meantime, a short presentation provides a brief introduction to Proxmox VE's features, as illustrated in the preceding screenshot.

When the installation is complete, you'll be prompted to click on **Next** one last time. The system will then begin to shut down and reboot, and may prompt you to remove the installation media:

```
0
[    1.991853] acpi PNP0C80:02: add_memory failed
[    1.991854] acpi PNP0C80:02: acpi_memory_enable_device() error
Proxmox startup
mounting proc filesystem
mounting sys filesystem
comandline: BOOT_IMAGE=/boot/linux26 ro ramdisk_size=16777216 rw quiet splash=silent
loading drivers:  shpchp i2c_piix4 pata_acpi mptspi 8250_fintek floppy mac_hid input_leds serio_raw psmouse pcspkr aesni_intel g
hash_clmulni_intel crc32_pclmul crct10dif_pclmul kvm_intel intel_powerclamp x86_pkg_temp_thermal intel_rapl
[    4.052395] piix4_smbus 0000:00:07.3: SMBus Host Controller not enabled!
[    4.405112] sd 2:0:0:0: [sda] Assuming drive cache: write through
modprobe: ERROR: could not insert 'ghash_clmulni_intel': Invalid argument
modprobe: ERROR: could not insert 'intel_powerclamp': No such device
modprobe: ERROR: could not insert 'x86_pkg_temp_thermal': No such device
[    4.518488] intel_rapl: no valid rapl domains found in package 0
modprobe: ERROR: could not insert 'intel_rapl': No such device
searching for cdrom
testing cdrom /dev/sr0
found proxmox cdrom
Starting Proxmox installation
Installing additional hardware drivers
[ ok ] Starting the hotplug events dispatcher: udevd.
[ ok ] Synthesizing the initial hotplug events...done.
[....] Waiting for /dev to be fully populated...[    5.364469] Error: Driver 'pcspkr' is already registered, aborting...
[    5.806894] intel_rapl: no valid rapl domains found in package 0
[    5.826773] intel_rapl: no valid rapl domains found in package 0
done.
Detecting network settings... done
Installation done, rebooting...
[....] Deconfiguring network interfaces...Killed old client process
Internet Systems Consortium DHCP Client 4.3.1
Copyright 2004-2014 Internet Systems Consortium.
All rights reserved.
For info, please visit https://www.isc.org/software/dhcp/

can't create /var/lib/dhcp/dhclient.eth0.leases: Read-only file system
Listening on LPF/eth0/00:0c:29:60:3e:ec
Sending on   LPF/eth0/00:0c:29:60:3e:ec
Sending on   Socket/fallback
done.
[ ok ] Stopping the hotplug events dispatcher: udevd.
Deactivating swap...done.
umount: /dev/.static/dev: mountpoint not found
[  230.329293] sysrq: SysRq : Kill All Tasks
unmounting cdrom
eject: /dev/sr0: Input/output error
rebooting - please remove the CD
_
```

Post-installation reboot

When the machine finishes rebooting, your new Proxmox VE instance will be ready to be put to work:

```
-------------------------------------------------------------------------------
Welcome to the Proxmox Virtual Environment. Please use your web browser to
configure this server - connect to:

  https://192.168.1.31:8006/

-------------------------------------------------------------------------------

pve4-1 login: _
```

Proxmox VE upon the completion of reboot

 In `Chapter 2`, *Installing Proxmox VE*, we'll access Proxmox VE through its administrative web interface via the URL displayed by the console by pointing a browser to the URL displayed by the console upon logging in.

Congratulations, your enterprise-class hypervisor is installed and almost ready for action; before we get started on PVE containers with LXC, let's make sure the system is up to date.

Upgrading PVE from the command line

At the **login:** prompt, type `root` and press *Enter*; when the password prompt appears, enter the root user's password that you defined during the installation.

To optimize performance, maximize uptime, and keep the system secure, it's imperative that software patches are applied to Proxmox VE.

Assuming you're getting acquainted with Promox VE before committing to a support subscription, a change must be made to the software repositories.

To update and upgrade PVE when it's not attached to a support subscription, the following steps are necessary:

1. Disable the enterprise repository.
2. Add a new repository called `no-subscription`.
3. Use `apt` to update the list of available packages.
4. Use `apt` to upgrade installed packages if upgrades exist.
5. Upgrade the distribution with `apt`.

Disabling the enterprise repository

Without this step, `apt-get update` will fail as `apt` tries to access the enterprise repo. So, we'll comment out the enterprise repo in the list of repositories:

```
sed -i.bak 's|deb https://enterprise.proxmox.com/debian jessie pve-
enterprise|\# deb https://enterprise.proxmox.com/debian jessie pve-
enterprise|' /etc/apt/sources.list.d/pve-enterprise.list
```

Enabling a non-subscriber repository

Although it's not intended for production use, **Proxmox GmbH** provides an alternative repository for non-subscribers. To enable it, create a new file in `/etc/apt/sources.list.d/` and write the repository information to it:

```
echo "deb http://download.proxmox.com/debian jessie pve-no-
subscription" > /etc/apt/sources.list.d/pve-no-sub.list
```

Visit `https://pve.proxmox.com/wiki/Package_repositories` to learn more about Proxmox VE package repositories.

Updating and upgrading Proxmox VE

Enter the following to get a fresh list of available packages in the repositories:

```
apt-get update
```

When the update has finished, use `apt` to get upgrades for your system:

```
apt-get upgrade -y
```

After that, try a distribution upgrade:

```
apt-get dist-upgrade -y
```

After the upgrade process is complete, reboot the server to ensure the changes are implemented:

```
shutdown -r now
```

Summary

In anticipation of the PVE installation process, this chapter first outlined how to download the Proxmox VE ISO. It made hardware recommendations based on the PVE documentation, and then offered a reminder to enable hardware virtualization on the target machine. It then provided a brief guide to enabling the extensions in EFI and BIOS.

To complete the preparations, you were encouraged to plan how you will respond to the Proxmox Installer's configuration prompts.

We then turned to the installation itself, moving through the Proxmox Installer one stage at a time.

With the conclusion of this chapter, you should have a fresh Proxmox VE installation waiting for you to begin work with `Chapter 3`, *Creating Containers*.

With the path appropriately paved, let's start building containers from templates.

3
Creating Containers

"Containers within a single operating system are much more efficient, and because of this efficiency, they underpin the future of the cloud infrastructure industry in place of VM architecture…Efficiency demands a future of containers running bare-metal hardware. Virtual machines have had their decade."

– Linux Journal, June 7, 2013

(http://www.linuxjournal.com/content/containers%E2%80%94not-virtual-machines%E2%80%94are-future-cloud)

"Everything at Google runs in a container….we start over 2 billion containers per week."

– Joe Beda, a senior staff software engineer for Google Cloud Platform in a talk at Gluecon 2014

(http://www.enterprisetech.com/2014/05/28/google-runs-software-containers/)

"If you're in data-center or cloud IT circles, you've been hearing about containers in general and Docker in particular non-stop for over a year now. With the release of Docker 1.0 in June, the buzz has become a roar."

– ZDNET, August 4, 2014

In Chapter 2, *Installing Proxmox VE*, we walked together through the Proxmox VE installation process.

This chapter's focus is creating containers from OS templates or virtual appliance templates. By its conclusion, this chapter will have addressed how to obtain templates and derive LXC containers from them with Proxmox VE. Along the way, we'll cover the following subjects:

- The advantages of, and an example use case for, containers
- Logging in to the Proxmox VE web-based management interface
- Exploring the OS templates and virtual appliances available directly through the management interface
- Creating a container from both the web-based interface and the command line
- Starting a new container from the management interface
- Changing a container's state directly through the PVE console or via the web-based administration interface

Understanding the container advantage

`Chapter 1`, *Proxmox VE Fundamentals*, introduced GNU/Linux containers generally and worked particularly at distinguishing them from virtual machines. This section elaborates some advantages of containers, and it imagines a scenario ideal for container deployment.

Where an administrator could run 10-100 virtual machines on a physical host, she/he could run 100-1000 containers on the same host without compromising significantly on performance (`http://computerpcdeal.com/servers-dell-poweredge/news_2014-0 6-17-05-30-07-224.html`).

Containers may be thought of, initially, as very lightweight virtual machines, but with much lower overhead and the added value of simplified deployment.

Proxmox VE and the case for LXC

Containers are the legacy of FreeBSD jails and have enjoyed a kind of renaissance that has become an increasingly valuable cultural touchstone among computing professionals, particularly since the rise of Docker in June of 2014.

It's important to keep in mind that Docker was originally reliant on LXC, or Linux Containers, the same technology that Proxmox VE relies on for its containerization layer since the release of 4,0.

Previous releases, in fact, relied on OpenVZ, another open source container technology. OpenVZ had a reputation for stability and reliability; in stark contrast, until very recently, LXC was described as a kind of young upstart, one with so much promise, but that was nevertheless still immature.

We see the rapid increase in currency that LXC has enjoyed, which is illustrated in the following screenshot of a Google Trends analysis at `https://www.google.com/trends/explore#q=%2Fm%2F0crds9p%2C%20OpenVZ&cmpt=q&tz=Etc%2FGMT%2B5`. As a search term, OpenVZ enjoys a very sharp increase in 2006, and its popularity is sustained until about 2009 before it starts to drop off.

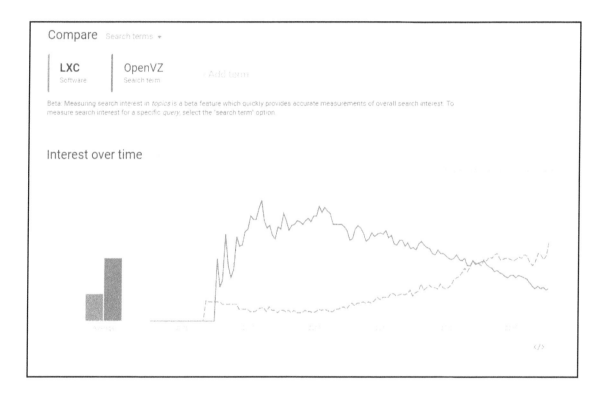

Interest over time for LXC and OpenVZ from Google Trends

Meanwhile, LXC slowly grows in popularity, until 2014 — the same year that Docker created a bit of a container uproar — LXC surpasses OpenVZ.

With the excitement and anxiety that this container renaissance provoked, it makes sense that Proxmox VE turned to LXC for its containerization layer in late 2015; it was cutting edge, it stabilized, and it had the support of contributors from corporations such as IBM and Canonical.

Terms that are very often interchangeable with containerization, in this context, include **OS virtualization** and **virtual private servers**.

For an infographic covering the history of containers—beginning with Unix V7 and tracing developments through 2014, visit `http://pivotal.io/platform/infographic/moments-in-container-history`.

Do note that Proxmox VE 4.1 ships with tools with which OpenVZ containers can be migrated to LXC. To learn more, visit the PVE wiki at `https://pve.proxmox.com/wiki/Convert_OpenVZ_to_LXC`.

Much like a VM, a container is an isolated entity; it can be independently rebooted, allowed isolated root access, and have a unique set of users and groups.

That same isolation also means, potentially, independent IP addresses, memory, processes, libraries, and configuration files.

LXC's feature set distinguishes it from full virtualization solutions:

- CPU resources spent on virtualization by the LXC containerization layer will be significantly lower than with full virtualization
- An authorized container user can change any configuration file and install additional software within a container without interfering with other containers or the Proxmox VE host
- While containers are fully isolated from each other, they do share dynamic libraries with the host, which greatly saves on RAM
- Most containers fully boot in seconds, while virtual machines may boot in minutes, on the same resources
- Because all containers run on the OS kernel of the host system, containers run with near-zero overhead
- Any container's network traffic is isolated from every other container; traffic snooping between containers is impossible
- Firewalling may be used inside a container, as may routing manipulation

In practical terms, these features suggest, for example, that containers can be scaled without a restart, and offer improved service efficiency and better performance than virtual machines, generally speaking.

It is absolutely worth noting that cautious pundits now suggest the celebrated performance advantage of containers and the decreased resources they demand is a diminishing advantage, particularly as more powerful hardware becomes available at a lower price. The argument here is that full virtualization still has a place, and that the benefit of containers is spectral so long as it argues from the perspective that hardware resources are scarce.

There's truth to this, but it doesn't negate the assertion that in many cases containers can be a less costly alternative to virtual machines without compromising on the quality of service.

Consider that the advantages articulated previously can directly lead to a longer lifespan for the physical host, as well as flexibility such that containers can be transferred quickly to another physical host to facilitate hardware maintenance; security is improved against certain threat types; and finally, LXC enjoys a thriving community of developers and users, a great resource for support that's available with or without a premium Proxmox VE subscription.

Container security

Chapter 7, *Secure Your Servers*, will focus particularly on virtual machine security.

While we're certainly in the thrall of a container revolution, there're still outstanding questions about container security and we must be diligent about pursuing questions. The LXC documentation at `https://linuxco ntainers.org/lxc/security/` offers some insight. More information is available from SANS Institute at `https://www.sans.org/reading-roo m/whitepapers/linux/securing-linux-containers-36142`, and finally, IBM offers some clear guidance at `http://www.ibm.com/develo perworks/library/l-lxc-security/`.

Nevertheless, in the domain of full virtualization, there are a variety of documents that work toward establishing a security protocol for virtual machines, regardless of the vendor. This gives us information to respond to and with which to develop a dialog.

Regrettably, this revolution is still young, and no such standards for OS-level virtualization seem readily available yet.

This very distinguished feature-set should provoke us to imagine a representative use case for LXC containers immediately; imagine the secondary education institution as a whole, then consider its various computing courses. The potential for consolidation of hardware resources for the two related scenarios is tremendous.

Computing and information and communication technology students, for example, can each have their own virtual private server with which to experiment and complete guided and independent practice. Each have their own virtual private servers with which to experiment, find inspiration, complete assessments, and realize their innovative visions.

Moreover, that same physical hardware could host a container each for relevant applications:

- A **learning management system** (**LMS**), such as *Moodle*
- A contained social network provided by a web application, such as *Elgg* (`https://elgg.org/about.php`)
- A microblogging system, such as *GNU Social* (`http://gnu.io/social/`)
- A directory server, such as *openLDAP*, to provide a single sign-on service across each platform
- A portfolio system with *Mahara* (`https://mahara.org/`)
- A web filter and firewall solution to protect not only the students, but also the integrity of the data, and confidentiality of the stakeholders, and availability of services
- A domain controller could be added for additional flexibility and functionality (`https://www.turnkeylinux.org/domain-controller`)

There's a hitch to containers; they're not a solution for every problem. For example, LXC, the container technology beneath PVE containers, only works with GNU/Linux guests.

Proxmox VE hosts further limit what Linux distributions are supported for containers. At present, these are the supported distributions and releases:

- Debain (6, 7 , 8)
- CentOS 6
- Ubuntu (12.04, 14.04, 15.04)
- Archlinux

This is mentioned with an absolute acknowledgement that 4.1 is a very recent release of PVE, and it's very clear that Proxmox VE will support more distributions with every passing month.

The next section is committed to the very first step required for us to provide services with containers hosted on PVE—obtaining container templates.

We'll close this section as a reminder that Proxmox VE is an enterprise-class virtualization platform that supports both containers and full virtualization—precisely because both have a role in the infrastructure.

Container templates

A template is the starting point for an LXC container (abbreviated in Proxmox VE as "CT"). There are two sorts of templates: **OS templates** and **appliance templates**.

OS templates provide a minimal set of packages from a GNU/Linux distribution, as well as system libraries and scripts, to start up and run the container. They're designed to benefit fully from the GNU/Linux kernel running on the host.

Aside from basic tools, such as a bash interpreter and utilities, additional software, such as a compiler or a DBMS is not usually incorporated into an OS template.

In contrast to OS templates, virtual appliances are built on top of JeOS (Just enough Operating System) to provide a very specific service reliably, securely, and with an absolute commitment to efficiency.

Virtual appliances can provide general functionality, such as LAMP stack; or a specific application, such as GitLab (`https://about.gitlab.com/`); a CMS such as WordPress or Drupal; or a web-based network monitoring system such as Observium (`http://www.obs ervium.org/`).

The most compelling aspect of virtual appliances is that they just work with minimal configuration or requisite tuning by the user.

Both OS templates and virtual appliances are available via the Proxmox VE management interface. At this point, all the available appliances are provided by **TurnKeyGNU/Linux**; who provide access to over 190 appliances, from web applications to SDKs (software development kits), as well as administrative templates for monitoring network activity, providing LDAP or a Domain Controller, and many more.

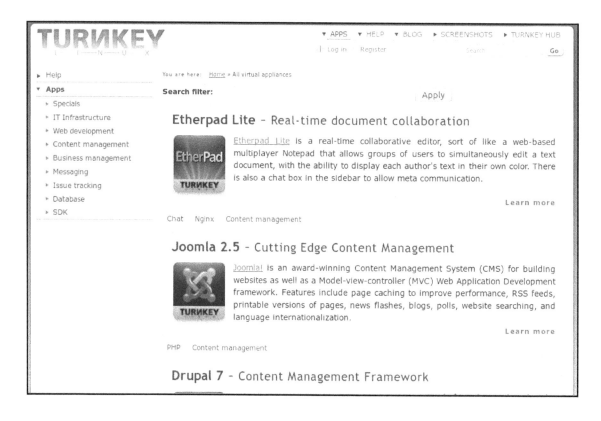

Website for the TurnKey GNU/Linux appliance library

Each of these appliances is built from the same JeOS version of Debian, called Turnkey GNU/Linux Core (Debian 8), and features at least shellinabox, OpenSSH server, and a customized Webmin.

TurnKey GNU/Linux Core
See `http://www.turnkeylinux.org/core` for more information on TurnKey GNU/Linux Core.

Downloading templates

Templates are available directly through the Proxmox VE management interface, which offers both OS templates and virtual appliance templates.

In this section, we'll login to the web-based management interface, navigate to storage in the server view, and then browse the list of available templates.

To follow along, your Proxmox VE host must be capable of accessing the Internet.

Logging in to Proxmox VE's web interface

To get started, login to Proxmox VE from a workstation on the same LAN; point a browser to port 8006 of the IP address of your Proxmox VE instance using SSL/TLS. The machine configured in this chapter has an address of `192.168.1.80`; to access this machine, for example, one can simply navigate to `https://192.168.1.80:8006` in a (JavaScript enabled) browser.

Because PVE has a self-signed certificate, the browser will warn that the connection can't be trusted. Firefox, for example, will present a window like this:

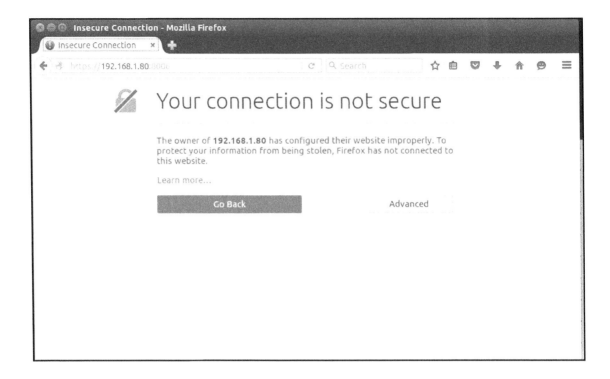

The Insecure Connection dialog (in Firefox)

Firefox users can proceed as follows:

1. To move forward in Firefox, select **Advanced** and click on the **Add Exception...** button that is revealed.

2. On the **Add Security Exception** dialog that pops up, click on **Confirm Security Exception** while noting that you may choose to store this exception permanently by selecting the **Permanently store this exception** check box (this dialog is captured in the following screenshot):

The Add Security Exception dialog (in Firefox)

If you're using Google Chrome to access the administrative interface, you should see a page similar to the following screenshot:

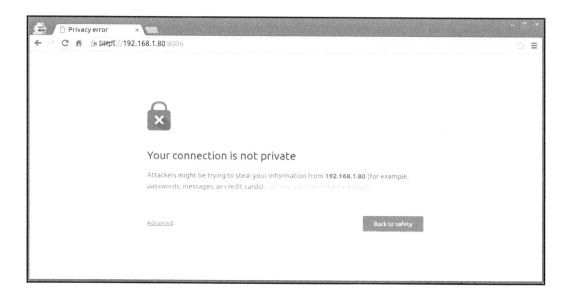

Privacy Error dialog in Google Chrome

To disregard this (somewhat discomforting) alert:

1. Scroll to the bottom of the page.
2. Click on **Advanced.**
3. Click on **Proceed to 192.168.1.80.**

Two things to note about this link: it is appended with "unsafe" as a reminder that this can be a security risk and of steps for chrome users.

Whichever browser is used, be sure to replace 192.168.1.80 with the IP address of your Proxmox VE host.

For explanations of these browser alerts, see the resources on self-signed certificates in relation to TLS/SSL:
http://en.wikipedia.org/wiki/Self-signed_certificate
http://en.wikipedia.org/wiki/HTTPS
http://security.stackexchange.com/questions/8110/what-are
-the-risks-of-self-signing-a-certificate-for-ssl

When the page loads completely, proceed to login with username `root` and the password that you determined during installation in `Chapter 2`, *Installing Proxmox VE.*

Select the **Realm** called **Linux PAM Standard Authentication**. The final field determines the language of the web interface. Make the selection of your choice and click on **Login** to proceed.

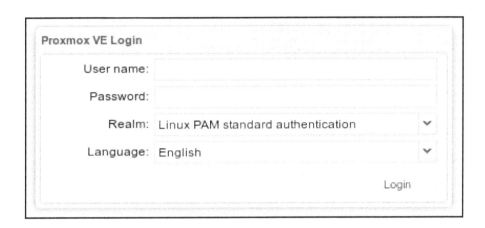

The login dialog for Proxmox VE web-management interface

After successfully logging in, you'll have your first view of the Proxmox VE administration GUI.

Browsing available container templates

In the left column, toward the banner, the selected view should already be set to **Server View**:

1. Expand the resource tree directly under **Server View** (the Datacenter node). At the bottom of the resource tree in the left frame will be storage that's local to the physical host and labeled **local** followed by your hostname in parenthesis; in the following screenshot, the hostname is `pve4` and the storage node is simply labeled local (`pve4`).

2. Select the storage node local to your server; in the following screenshot, for example, select **local (pve4)**:

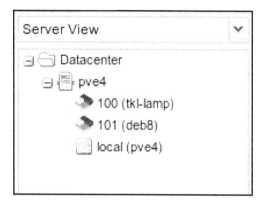

Server View and Resource Tree (expanded to reveal local (pve4))

3. Three tabs will appear in the right frame; **Summary**, **Content**, and **Permissions**.

Select the **Content** tab to reveal both a **Templates** button and an **Upload** button.

Local storage for the PVE node called pve4. Screenshot to visualize locations of local (PVE4), as well as the Templates and Upload buttons

To browse the list or download an OS template and virtual appliance provided through the PVE interface, follow these steps:

1. Click on the **Templates** tab.
2. Scroll through the pop-up browser window until you find a template that suits your interests.

Templates			✕
Type	Package ▲	Version	Description
⊟ Section: system (9 Items)			
lxc	archlinux-base	2015-24-29-1	ArchLinux base image.
lxc	centos-6-default	20150829	LXC default image for centos 6 (20150829)
lxc	centos-7-default	20150829	LXC default image for centos 7 (20150829)
lxc	debian-6.0-standard	6.0-7	Debian 6.0 (standard)
lxc	debian-7.0-standard	7.0-3	Debian 7.0 (standard)
lxc	debian-8.0-standard	8.0-1	Debian 8.0 (standard)
lxc	ubuntu-12.04-standard	12.04-1	Ubuntu Precise (standard)
lxc	ubuntu-14.04-standard	14.04-1	Ubuntu Trusty (standard)
lxc	ubuntu-15.04-standard	15.04-1	Ubuntu Vivid (standard)
⊟ Section: turnkeylinux (96 Items)			
lxc	turnkey-ansible	14.0-1	TurnKey Ansible
lxc	turnkey-asp-net-apache	14.0-1	TurnKey ASP .Net on Apache
lxc	turnkey-b2evolution	14.0-1	TurnKey b2evolution
lxc	turnkey-bugzilla	14.0-1	TurnKey Bugzilla
lxc	turnkey-cakephp	14.0-1	TurnKey CakePHP
lxc	turnkey-canvas	14.0-1	TurnKey Canvas LMS
lxc	turnkey-codeigniter	14.0-1	TurnKey CodeIgniter
lxc	turnkey-collabtive	14.0-1	TurnKey Collabtive
lxc	turnkey-concrete5	14.0-1	TurnKey Concrete5
lxc	turnkey-core	14.0-1	TurnKey Core
lxc	turnkey-couchdb	14.0-1	TurnKey CouchDB
lxc	turnkey-django	14.0-1	TurnKey Django
lxc	turnkey-dokuwiki	14.0-1	TurnKey DokuWiki
			Download

A glimpse at a few of the container templates available through the Proxmox VE interface

Turnkey GNU/Linux Appliance Library
If you decide you want to know more about a particular Turnkey GNU/Linux appliance, point your browser to `http://www.turnkelin ux.org/all` and have a look at the elaborated description and feature lists for each appliance.

Downloading a container

For the remainder of the chapter, I'll be working with the Ubuntu 14.04-standard template. While it's recommended that you follow along, there are many exciting templates to start from.

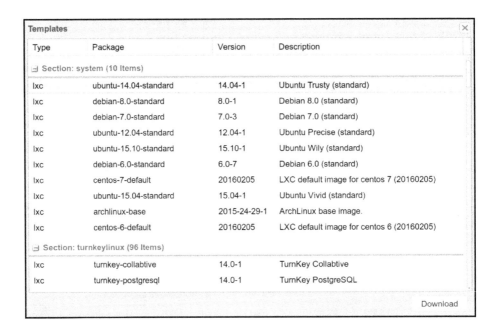

Preparing to create a Ubuntu 14.04.1 container

Once you've selected an OS or appliance template:

1. Click to select your choice.
2. Click on the **Download** button.

The template will be saved to PVE's local storage in `/usr/share/vz/cache/templates/`.

> If the list of available templates in the web interface seems incomplete, it can be refreshed from the command line of the PVE host. Access the command line interface by logging on to the host locally, via SSH, or using the noVNC console available on the web interface.
> After authenticating, refresh the list of templates by simply entering `pveam` at the prompt.

Now that a template is downloaded, a container can be built from it. In the next section, we'll configure and create the first template.

From template to container

You may have noted that when you've highlighted an item in storage—ISO or template, the option to **Create CT** (container) or **Create VM** (virtual machine) appears at the top of the right-hand frame. To build a container from a template with Proxmox VE:

1. Have, at least, the following information ready:

    - A password for the root user
    - A name for the host
    - A free IPv4 address for the host
    - Max amount of RAM
    - CPU count
    - An idea of the storage space you want for the (virtual) hard drive (in GB)
    - The IPv4 address of the internet gateway
    - The appropriate subnet mask of the network the host is on

2. Once you're certain of this information, select the template in local that you want to build a container from.
3. Click on the **Create CT** button at the top right (see the following screenshot).

Create CT and VM to appear at the top of the right-hand corner

4. Clicking on **Create CT** will start the **Create LXC Container** dialog, which provides a GUI for configuring the container.

   The first tab is **General**:

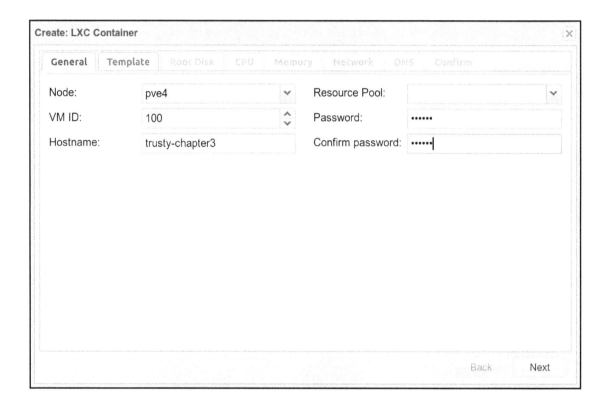

The General tab of the container creation dialog

Use this dialog to define the hostname and confirm the password of the root user. The VM ID field auto-populates and auto-increments in the Web interface: the first guest created will have a default **VM ID** of 100, the next 101, and so on.

5. Click on **Next** to proceed to the **Template** tab, illustrated here:

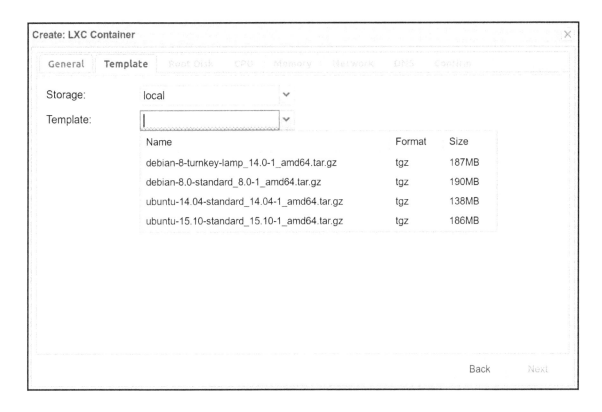

The Template tab of the container creation dialog

6. To follow this text, choose **Ubuntu-14.04-standard_14.04-1_amd64.tar.gz** from the drop-down **Template** menu and click **Next** to continue to the **Root Disk** tab.

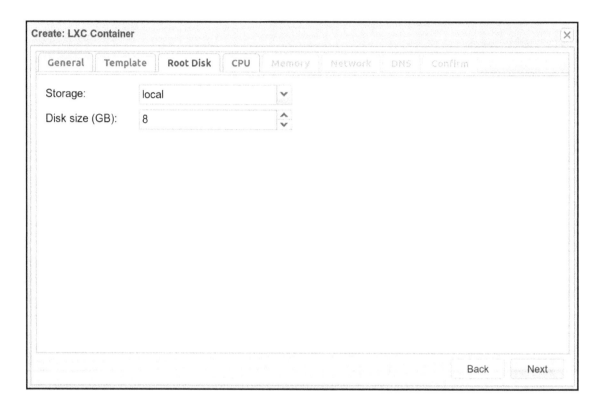

The Root Disk tab of the container creation dialog

At this stage, **Storage** is defined as **local** and there are no alternatives available. Define the size of the virtual disk for the container to suit your preferences (but work to avoid a **Disk Size** of less than 4 GB).

7. Click on **Next** to define a **CPU** limit and units for the container. For the purpose of this text, let's leave these settings at the default.

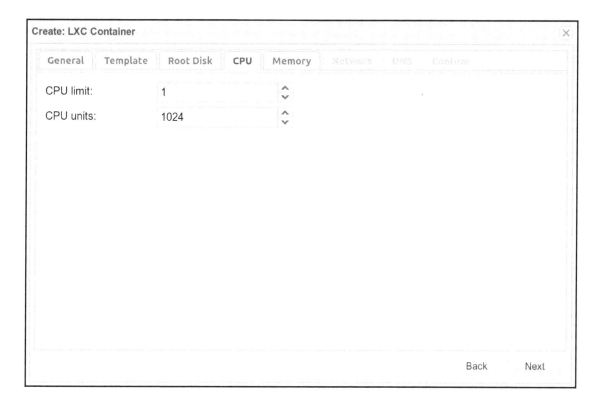

The CPU tab of the container creation dialog

8. Click on **Next** to configure **Memory** for the container.

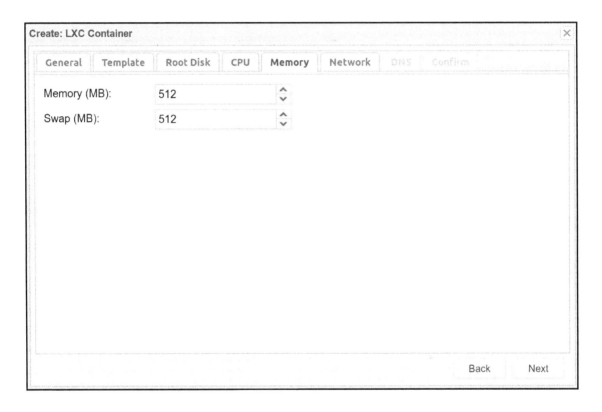

The Memory tab of the container creation dialog

9. Once again, the defaults are good for our purposes, so we'll move forward from the **Memory** tab onto the **Network** tab:

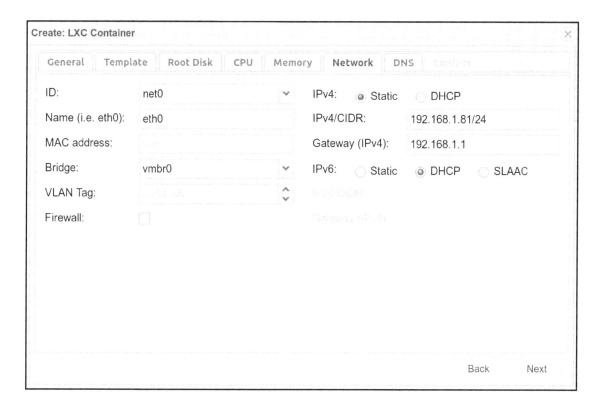

The Network tab of the container creation dialog

The **Network** tab assumes some prior knowledge about the configuration of the network the container is joining. Since the PVE host is at `192.168.1.80` in this case, this first container will be addressed as `192.168.1.81`, a static address I'm confident won't conflict with other devices. Static is selected instead of DHCP at the top right of the tab.

Be sure to indicate the scope in the **IPv4/CIDR** field. In this case, the subnet mask is 255.255.255.0, so the IP address is appended with `/24`. If the correct subnet mask for the network included more addresses, as 255.255.0.0 would, simply append `/16` instead, for example. For those of us who don't have the CIDR notation at the ready, there's a calculator available at `http://www.subnet-calculator.com/cidr.php`.

For our purposes, **IPv6** isn't of concern; choose the **DHCP** radio button and then check out the left column of the **Network** tab.

Name refers to how the virtual network interface will appear inside the container; the default, **eth0**, is precisely what we want.

The **Bridge** field asks which bridge on the host to connect the container to. In the preceding screenshot, vmbr0 is the default, and only, choice; the machine I'm using has only one NIC, and it is defined in the host as vmbr0.

When ready to commit the settings in the **Network** tab, click on **Next** to point the container to a DNS server.

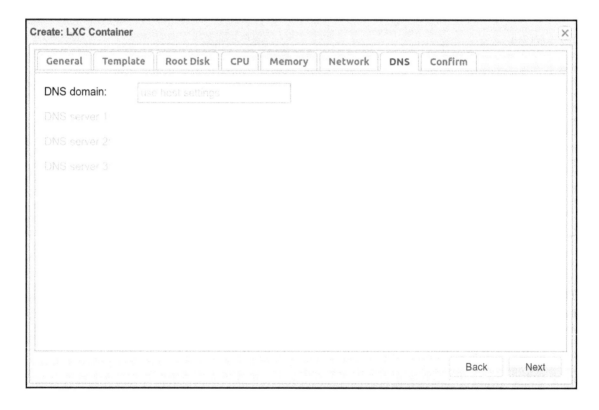

The DNS tab of the container creation dialog

Again, in the case of my network, the default setting in which the **DNS domain** field is set to **use host settings** is a perfect fit. To review and commit the configuration, click on **Next**.

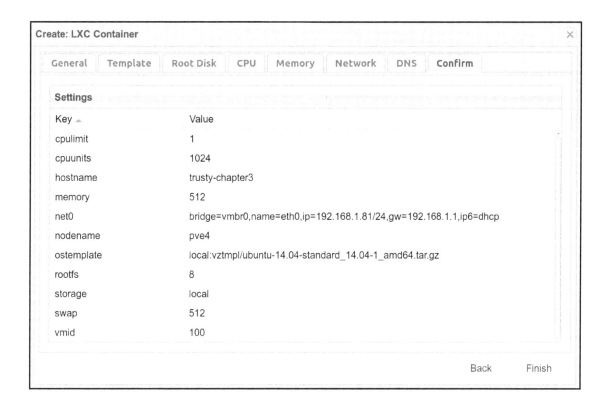

The Confirm tab in the container creation dialog

The **Confirm** tab offers a configuration summary, as well as an opportunity the revisit some configuration decisions. Click on **Back** to make adjustments or **Finish** to begin the container creation task.

As soon as **Finish** is clicked, the configuration dialog closes and a new window opens in the browser that offers an opportunity to watch PVE build the LXC container from the template based on your configuration:

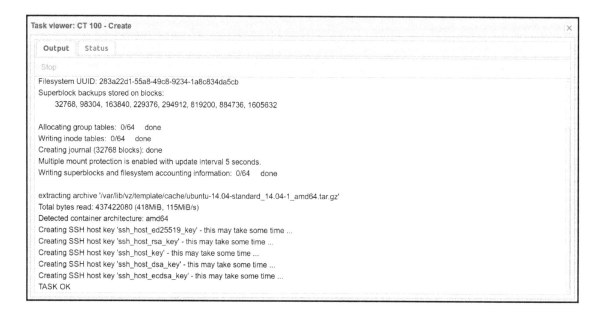

Task viewer: CT 100 - Create ×

Output	**Status**

Stop

Filesystem UUID: 283a22d1-55a8-49c8-9234-1a8c834da5cb
Superblock backups stored on blocks:
    32768, 98304, 163840, 229376, 294912, 819200, 884736, 1605632

Allocating group tables: 0/64   done
Writing inode tables: 0/64   done
Creating journal (32768 blocks): done
Multiple mount protection is enabled with update interval 5 seconds.
Writing superblocks and filesystem accounting information: 0/64   done

extracting archive '/var/lib/vz/template/cache/ubuntu-14.04-standard_14.04-1_amd64.tar.gz'
Total bytes read: 437422080 (418MiB, 115MiB/s)
Detected container architecture: amd64
Creating SSH host key 'ssh_host_ed25519_key' - this may take some time ...
Creating SSH host key 'ssh_host_rsa_key' - this may take some time ...
Creating SSH host key 'ssh_host_key' - this may take some time ...
Creating SSH host key 'ssh_host_dsa_key' - this may take some time ...
Creating SSH host key 'ssh_host_ecdsa_key' - this may take some time ...
TASK OK

The output of Task viewer as the container creation completes

When the **Task viewer** window outputs TASK OK, the container is ready to use. The **Task viewer** window can be closed.

 A container can also be created from a template using a PVE host's command line using the pct create command. The following bash script illustrates the use of this command to create a container nearly identical to the one created through the web-based procedure detailed previously:

```
#!/bin/bash
#### Set Variables ####
$hostname="trusty-chapter3"
$vmid="100"
$template-path="/var/lib/vz/template/cache"
$storage="local"
$description="trusty container for Chapter 3"
$template=" Ubuntu-14.04-standard_14.04-1_amd64.tar.gz"
$ip="192.168.1.81/24"
$nameserver="8.8.8.8"
$ram="1024"
$rootpw="changeme"
$rootfs="4"
$gateway="192.168.1.1"
$bridge="vmbr0"
```

```
$if="eth0"
#### Execute pct create using variable substitution ####
pct create $vmid \
   $template-path/$template \
   -description $description \
   -rootfs $rootfs \
   -hostname $hostname \
   -memory $ram \
   -nameserver $nameserver \
   -storage $storage \
   -password $rootpw \
   -net0 name=$if,ip=$ip,gw=$gateway,bridge=$bridge
```

In most cases, making changes to a container's configuration and adding virtual devices is a simple matter that can be accomplished through the web interface. To edit the configuration or add devices:

1. Select the container in **Server** view in the left frame of the interface.
2. In the frame on the right, look below the **Start** button for a group of tabs (shown in the following screenshot).
3. Match the task you want to complete to the tab name.
4. Use the **Add** and **Edit** buttons to make the desired changes.

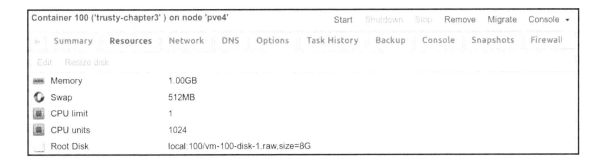

Most container configuration changes can be made through the PVE Web interface

The next section is about controlling the state of any given container; for example, how to start it and stop it.

Starting and stopping containers

To start the container, select it in the left pane; the icon should be black and gray, indicating a container that is not running.

1. In the following screenshot, my container is identified with a VM ID of **100** and the name **trusty-chapter3**:

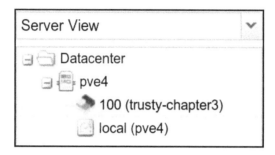

Icon of stopped container

2. In the upper-right corner of the interface, start the container by clicking on the **Start** button:

Container Start button

When the container start up process is complete, it is signified in the left frame of the interface by a change in the color of the container's icon; it should now be green, black, and grey instead of simply black and grey; the green addition to the icon is a quick way to visually distinguish a running container from a stopped one.

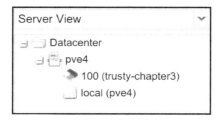

The icon of a running container is green, black, and grey

In the resource tree, in the left frame, select the running container.

On the right side of the screen, several buttons become available:

- Clicking on **Shutdown** will shut down the container gracefully
- The **Stop** button, by way of contrast, will halt the container abruptly
- **Migrate** allows us to move, even a running container between the Proxmox VE cluster nodes without causing any service outages or other downtime
- The **Remove** button will delete a stopped container. Note that there is no recovery option if the container is not backed up.

To suspend a container, choose the container's **Backup** tab in the PVE web interface. Click on **Backup now**, and in the dialog box that appears, select **Suspend** from the **Mode** drop-down menu. Click on the **Backup** button to suspend the container and close the dialog.

Containers can be suspended from the PVE Web interface

Changing container states with the command line

A container's state may also be controlled from a PVE host's command line (whether via SSH session, noVNC console, or logged in to the physical host).

To start the container described in this chapter and assigned the VM ID of 100, enter `pct start 100`. Likewise, the same container can be brought down with `pct stop 100`.

Templates can be backed up from either the PVE command line or the web interface. To learn more about backing up and restoring containers, visit the Proxmox wiki at `https://pve.proxmox.com/wiki/Linux_Container#Backup_container`.

Accessing a container

Most OS templates available through Proxmox VE are initially configured to be accessed either through the noVNC console, which can be launched from the management web interface, or from the PVE command line interface.

That's not to say OpenSSH isn't installed; in fact, I haven't seen a template without the OpenSSH server installed. The OS templates simply aren't configured at launch so the root user can login with a password. (However, TurnKey Linux's appliances can be accessed through SSH by the root account using a password.)

The pct enter command makes it a breeze to access a container from the PVE host's command line interface. To enter the container developed in this chapter, I could access the PVE host via SSH, for example, by logging in as the root user; then, I could follow `pct enter` with the VM ID of the container, which in this case is `100`. Simply type `pct enter 100` at the prompt and press *Enter* to drop into a shell within the container.

To access a running container through the **noVNC** console, select the running template in the web interface, and then select **Console** at the top right of the browser, and select **noVNC** from the drop-down menu.

When a started container is selected, the Console button appears in the top-right corner of the page

Alternatively, select the running template as described previously, but instead of clicking on the **Console** drop-down menu, choose the **Console** tab for the container.

If you have access to a terminal via the console, as illustrated in the following screenshot, you're all set to create users, install packages, and make other configuration changes to make the container your own.

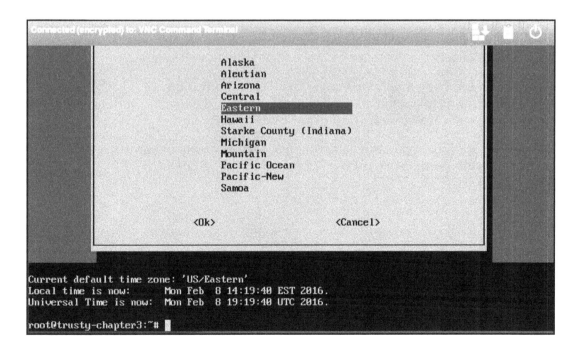

Reconfiguring a Ubuntu container's time-zone data from noVNC console session

If the console launches but displays only a black screen and an unresponsive cursor, try pressing *Enter* and look for a log in prompt. If that doesn't work, consider that some containers have to be restarted once to prompt for credentials; restart the container and then once more, launch the noVNC console. If the noVNC screen is still dark, press *Enter* to finesse a prompt from it.

 You'll want to configure locales and the time zone for most containers. `dpkg-reconfigure locales` will lead you through a brief dialog to determine which locales are available on a Debian or Ubuntu container. `dpkg-reconfigure tzdata` will lead you through the necessary steps to setup or reconfigure the time zone data for a Debian or Ubuntu container.

Summary

This chapter detailed the process of developing containers from LXC templates. We explored the promise of LXC containers in Proxmox VE, and outlined an example use case that could be generalized to other circumstances and that demonstrated how the Proxmox VE container's features could add value, flexibility, and extensibility to an organization's IT infrastructure.

After describing how to derive a container from a template, we explored ways to manipulate containers from both the command line and the web interface.

In `Chapter 4`, *Creating Virtual Machines*, we will identify advantages of virtual machines over containers and explore some use cases. At the close of the chapter, we'll have walked through the creation of Microsoft Windows and GNU/Linux virtual machines from ISOs.

With what we know now about containers, it'll be exciting to explore the place for virtual machines in a culture whose fascination is fixed on containerization.

4
Creating Virtual Machines

"…But if the concept of abstraction is so mundane in IT, what explains the increasing fascination with virtualization in recent years? The trend is even more hard-core in data centers, where virtualization is deeply ingrained in the development strategy of these environments since the mid-2000s. And the infatuation continues to grow….Accordingly, these facilities have been assaulted with virtual servers, virtual networks, virtual storage, virtual appliances, and other "V-technologies" that promise relief from the cuffs of reality."

– Gustavo A. A. Santana, *Data Center Virtualization Fundamentals*

In Chapter 3, *Creating Containers*, we explored the creation, configuration, and control of LXC containers using Proxmox VE. In this chapter, we turn our focus to KVM-QEMU virtual machine creation and control with Proxmox VE.

While we contrasted virtual machines with containers in Chapter 1, *Proxmox VE Fundamentals*, we will take this opportunity to dive deeper into specific advantages virtual machines still seem to have over containers despite the clear signs that we're in the thrall of a container revolution. At the same time, we will explore use cases based on what we've learned.

We will then walk through the process of deriving virtual machines from ISO images using Proxmox VE. PVE is intended as a server virtualization platform; therefore, we'll walk through the creation and configuration of two VMs: the first running Microsoft Windows 2012r2 and the second running Fedora Core 23 Server.

Since both operating systems have graphical user interface components, we will take advantage of an opportunity to explore more of the PVE's feature set than we might otherwise have had an authentic need to cover.

By the conclusion of `Chapter 4`, *Creating Virtual Machines*, we'll have covered the following aspects of full virtualization with Proxmox VE:

- Uploading ISOs to Proxmox VE's local storage
- Creating and configuring virtual machines from the PVE web interface
- Interacting with VMs using the PVE web interface's console feature
- Reconfiguring a virtual machine
- Controlling the state of a virtual machine

First, however, we will take a step back and explore the persistent role hardware virtualization will have, even as enthusiasm for containers echoes around us.

Distinguishing features of virtual machines

Though containers have clearly gained impressive momentum in so brief a period, virtual machines continue to have salient and distinguishing features. For example:

- A VM may run any operating system designed for the host's architecture; for example, Android-x86, FreeBSD, Ubuntu, Windows Server, and even desktop OSs can all run on separate virtual machines on a Proxmox VE host, provided the host has adequate hardware resources.

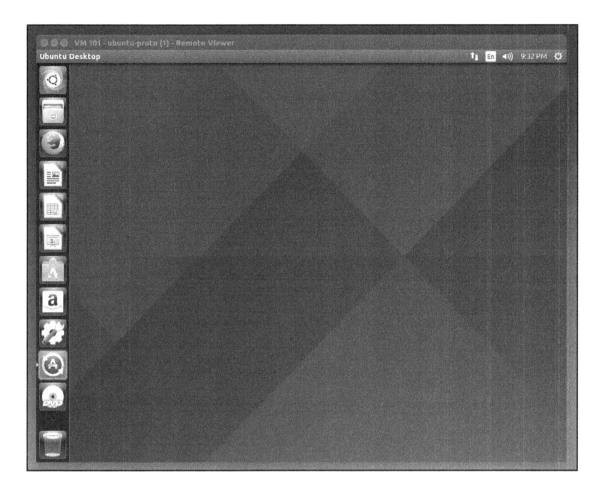

Ubuntu 15.04 virtual machine hosted on Proxmox VE and accessed via the SPICE console option in the PVE's Web interface

- One VM may host many containers; when we look for creative and savvy data center solutions, we would like to stay consistently aware that OS virtualization and system virtualization have a complementary relationship, rather than a competitive or antagonistic one. VMs still offer more thorough isolation, for example, than containers.
- VMs and containers call for different security concerns and approaches. Impressively thorough standards for system virtualization are mature and freely available, while intelligence on OS virtualization security and standardized solutions are not yet mature.

We'll address security and PVE more thoroughly in `Chapter 7`, *Securing Proxmox VE.*

System virtualization's distinguishing features suggest that, for the time being, virtual machines are more flexible than containers; for example, many operating systems may coexist on a single **hypervisor** such as Proxmox VE. Containers cannot achieve this. For now, this means that pure containers will only exist when GNU-/Linux-based hosts have GNU-/Linux-based containers and Microsoft-based containers can only run on Microsoft OS-based hosts. Containers hosted by Proxmox VE thus require that the host OS share GNU/Linux libraries and binaries.

With as much momentum as the container movement has, this restriction of containers to Unix-type operating systems may change very soon with the release of Windows Server 2016, which is now available to preview; Microsoft has announced plans to incorporate Docker into the product (`http://zdnet.com/article/microsoft-to-add-virtualiz ed-containers-non-server-mode-to-windows-server-2016/`, accessed June 1, 2015).

Docker is an open-source containerization solution under very active development and that is generating significant attention. A brief investigation suggests that a Windows host running Docker can run Linux containers. This counterpoint is quickly resolved once we realize Docker actually does this only with the support of a system virtualization layer, such as boot2docker (`https://github.com/boot2docker/boot2docke r`).

The flexibility system virtualization may claim, with regard to operating systems, does come at a cost: *virtual machines require more resources and have more overhead than containers.*

In the next section, we'll explore scenarios that make system virtualization nevertheless compelling.

Scenarios for system virtualization

From the distinguishing features discussed previously, some very powerful use cases emerge. For example:

- Cross-platform software development and testing
- Administration and management of systems in an enterprise with concerns across platforms
- Dependency on legacy applications, systems, or data
- A proving ground for deployment of new systems or policies
- Labs serving IT and ICT students
- Productivity and consistency across platforms

These scenarios highlight the changes brought about by each difference, particularly between the two forms of virtualization encouraged and supported by Proxmox VE, virtual machines, and containers.

This chapter proceeds with confidence to an informed conclusion: containers and virtual machines (or OS virtualization and system virtualization) are two different tools that together provide the data center and its engineers with powerful flexibility and an opportunity to exercise discretion in the (re)formation of the datacenter.

Let's have a look at the VM creation process with Proxmox VE.

Creating a virtual machine

This section provides an abstract overview of the virtual machine creation process, from configuring the machine to the installation of the operating system and ultimately to controlling its state.

Installation media

In the best-case scenario, the operating system intended for a new virtual machine is available as a downloadable ISO file. This single file is intended to perfectly represent an entire CD or DVD. In the case of several GNU/Linux distributions, the full install media spans several DVDs.

Usually, in these cases, a network installation (or `netinst`) disk image is available that provides just enough operating system to drive the system devices, the installer, and then download and install requested software from online repositories.

When the OS is available as an ISO, we can simply download it to a remote workstation and then upload it to the PVE host's local storage using PVE's web interface, and carry on with the creation of the VM.

Uploading an ISO file to local storage on PVE

There are five steps to working with an ISO image from a remote workstation.

1. Download the ISO from the Web to a local workstation and verify that the image is not corrupted or compromised (see `http://www.online-tech-tips.com/cool-websites/what-is-checksum/` to learn more about this process).

2. Access the Proxmox VE web interface by navigating to it in a browser (point your browser to `https://<ip address>:8006`, where `<ipaddress>` is the IP address of PVE).

3. In the left pane of the browser window, **Server View** should be selected. Beneath the drop-down menu, a folder labeled **Datacenter** should be available. Expand the contents to reveal your PVE host, labeled by hostname. Expand that to reveal the host's local storage, and then select its local storage. In the following screenshot, for example, the hostname of the PVE host is pve4, so the local storage is labeled **local (pve4)**.

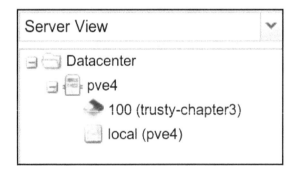

Navigating to a PVE node's local storage

4. After choosing local storage, three tabs should appear in the right
   pane: **Summary**, **Content**, and **Permissions**. Select the **Content** tab to reveal two
   buttons in the right pane, **Templates** and **Uploads**:

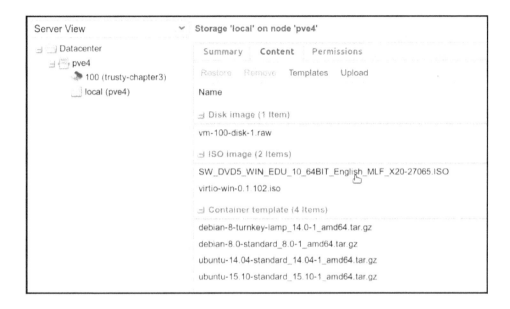

Local storage

5. To proceed, click on the **Upload** button. In the dialog that appears, choose **ISO
   image** from the drop-down menu labeled **Content**, then click on the **Select File…**
   button to browse the workstation's filesystem for the disk image to be uploaded
   to the PVE host.

Upload dialog

The path to the ISO files uploaded to PVE's local storage via its web interface is `/var/lib/template/iso` by default. With this in mind, note that files can also be transferred to this location from a workstation via `scp` or `sftp` to the Proxmox VE server, provided the tools are installed on the remote workstation.

With the install media available to PVE, we're ready to configure and create a VM using Proxmox VE's web interface. The next section explores the process.

Preparing a virtual machine

We begin the process by finding the hostname and local storage of our Proxmox VE instance in the server view of the PVE web interface. Select the host and click on the **Create VM** button (at the upper right corner of the page) to start configuring a new virtual machine.

A dialog entitled **Create: Virtual Machine** appears in the browser window. This is used to provide initial specifications for the new virtual machine, including not only hardware specifications, but also the OS type and the name PVE will use to refer to the new VM.

The tabs, from left to right, are as follows:

- General
- OS
- CD/DVD
- Hard Disk
- CPU
- Memory
- Network
- Confirm

After completing a tab, move forward either by clicking on the next tab in the sequence or by clicking on the **Next** button.

Anticipating the configuration tabs

What follows is a brief overview of what we can expect from each tab in the **Create: Virtual Machine** dialog.

General

It's on the **General** tab that the name and VM ID of a virtual machine are defined. Note that the "name" field doesn't refer to the VM's hostname; that's defined when the OS is configured. Rather, it is the name that Proxmox VE will use to refer to this VM in the web interface.

In a production environment, it's recommended that you stay deliberate and systematic with your naming scheme, just as you would be with a hostname in a datacenter.

When defining the VM ID, it is similarly important to be rigorously systematic. Each VM and container must be assigned a unique number that PVE refers to as VM ID. Although Proxmox VE will provide a default VM ID number, this is an arbitrary system, rather than a deliberated system resulting from a well-formed policy.

In a large production environment, consider assigning VM IDs in a dedicated range relative to the virtual server's purpose (for example, VM ID 1000-2000 for VMs providing web services). You'll appreciate that you did if your datacenter grows as you systematize backup plans and establish a plan for virtual-server lifecycle management.

OS

The **OS** tab provides some support for creating VMs intended for use with specific operating systems. Note there are multiple options, based on the kernel version, for GNU/Linux distributions.

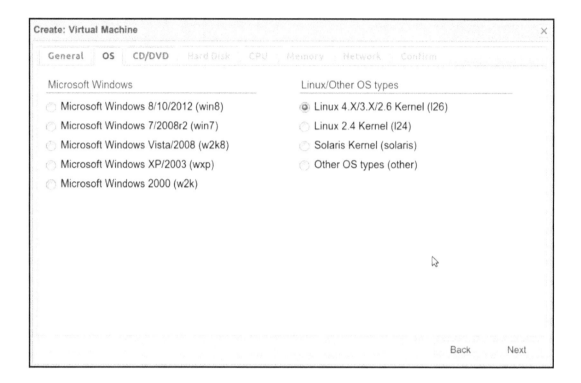

CD/DVD

The **CD/DVD** tab provides an opportunity to specify the initial disc image to be used for installing the OS; alternatively, we can direct PVE to rely on a physical disc in a local optical drive. If you select an ISO image, you're asked to choose from among the ISOs that are already uploaded to Proxmox VE.

Hard Disk

On the **Hard Disk** tab, we can define the size of the secondary storage allocated for the VM. There's also a **Bus/Device** field, as well as a field labeled **Storage** to specify the location to store the virtual disk. For the purpose of this text, we'll keep this field set to the default, **local**.

For more on virtual storage, see `Chapter 5,` *Working with Virtual Disks*.

CPU

The **CPU** tab provides an opportunity to define not only the CPU socket count, but also the number of cores to utilize per socket.

Memory

The **Memory** tab offers two methods for allocating RAM for the virtual machine; we can select a fixed amount in MB, or we can automatically allocate RAM within a specified range.

Network

Of particular interest on the Network tab are the three networking modes available in the left column of the tab and the opportunity to define the **Model** of the network interface in the right column.

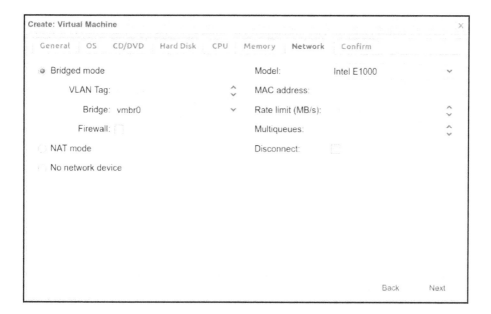

In the preceding screenshot, the VM will be configured to behave as if it's connected directly to the physical network by relying on PVE's bridged mode. By way of contrast, the NAT (network address translation) mode connects the VM to an isolated LAN maintained by the host and well isolated from the physical network.

In the same screenshot, the model of the network card is set to **Intel E1000**. Performance is not as good as we'd get from **virtio paravirtualization**, but Microsoft Windows guests will work out of the box with this model, whereas virtio would need additional drivers. Intel E1000 stands out for its compatibility, while virtio offers superior performance.

A VM configured with NAT mode can access resources on the physical network, but is not visible or accessible to resources beyond the Proxmox VE host.

Proxmox VE's network model is sophisticated and very flexible. To learn more, see Chapter 6, *Networking and Proxmox VE*, which is a chapter dedicated to Proxmox VE networking. Also, consider a visit to the wiki page https://pve.proxmox.com/wiki/Network_Model.

Confirm

The **Confirm** tab offers a summary view of the VM configuration to review before committing to the creation of the VM.

On this tab, a **Finish** button appears where the **Next** button was on the other tabs. To create the VM, click on the **Finish** button.

After completing the **Create: Virtual Machine** dialog, the virtual machine is configured—analogous to having built a physical computer, plugged it in, powered it up just long enough to insert your installation media in the optical drive, and then eagerly looking forward to it powering back on for the installation of the OS.

Stay conscious of the host's hardware specifications and cognizant of how resources are allocated as VMs and containers accumulate on a PVE host.

The next step is to start the newly created VM and install its operating system. First, let's step section steps through controlling the state of a virtual machine: starting it, shutting it down, and abruptly stopping it.

Controlling the state of a virtual machine

At this point in the process, the freshly created VM appears in **Server View** in a powered off state:

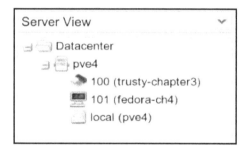

The icon of a VM that is stopped

In the preceding screenshot, the only VM on the host has a VM ID of 101 and the name fedora-ch4. A stopped VM is represented by a monitor icon with a black display.

If we select the VM in the left pane, buttons to control its state appear in the right pane, which is exactly what we saw with containers in the previous chapter:

Starting a VM

The **Start** button will "power on" the VM and the boot process will begin.

 A running VM is represented by a monitor icon with a white screen that visually distinguishes it from the icon for a stopped VM.

Once started, we can open the VM's noVNC console to see what's going on during the boot process, from the BIOS options through the OS's first interaction with the user. The same tool works for graphical user interfaces and command line interfaces.

Changing the state of a running VM

To stop a virtual machine gracefully, use the **Shutdown** button that becomes available upon start. Alternatively, use **Stop** to shut down a VM abruptly. The **Reset** button will halt the virtual machine, much as a hardware reset button would.

To destroy a virtual machine, ensure first that it is in a stopped state, then press the **Remove** button to reveal a concerned warning that the process initiated is not reversible. PVE will offer the choice to **Cancel** and give the action additional consideration, or to follow through with the destruction of the machine.

Controlling a VM from the PVE command line

The qm command allows us to control the state of a VM from a Proxmox VE command line interface. In the following examples, the changes will be made to the virtual machine with VM ID 101:

- qm destroy 101: This destroys the VM and deletes all of its used or owned volumes
- qm reset 101: This resets the VM
- qm resume 101: This resumes the VM (if it's suspended)
- qm shutdown 101: This shuts down the VM
- qm start 101: This starts the VM
- qm stop 101: This stops the VM
- qm suspend 101: This suspends the machine

 The qm command offers full control of a VM, from creation to destruction. To learn more, visit the manual page at https://pve.proxmox.com/wik i/Manual:_qm.

In the sections that follow, the abstract outline and illustration of the VM-creation and configuration process will become more concrete and specific as we apply what we learned to building two virtual machines: first we'll walk through the creation of a Windows Server 2012r2 VM, and then we'll create a Fedora 23 Server virtual machine.

Practicing the creation of virtual machines

In this section and the next, we'll run through the entire VM creation process, from the acquisition of ISO images, to the configuration of the machines, and the installation of the operating systems.

First, we'll step through the process for a Microsoft Windows Server 2012r2 system. Afterwards, we'll look at the creation of a VM intended for Fedora 23 Server.

Virtualizing Windows Server 2012r2 with Proxmox VE

If you want to precisely follow the installation process outlined here, it will require a Windows Server 2012r2 ISO image, perhaps from an existing DVD if necessary. If you have access to the Volume License Center, you're perhaps able to download the image file from Microsoft by visiting `https://www.microsoft.com/Licensing/servicecenter/default.aspx`.

At the time of writing, WindowsServer 2012r2 is available for evaluation (limited to 180 days) at Microsoft's TechNet Evaluation Center: `https://www.microsoft.com/en-us/evalcenter/evaluate-windows-server-2012-r2`.

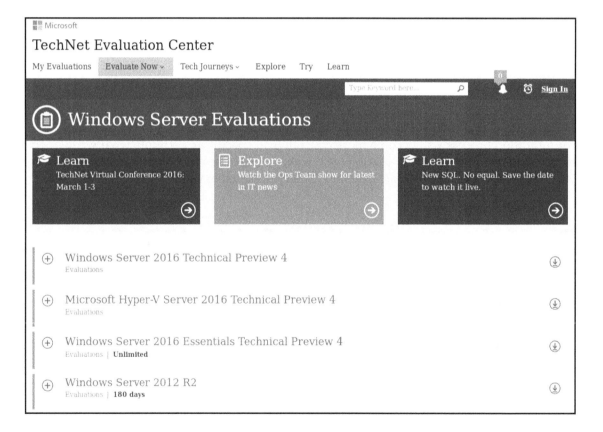

Microsoft's TechNet Evaluation Center

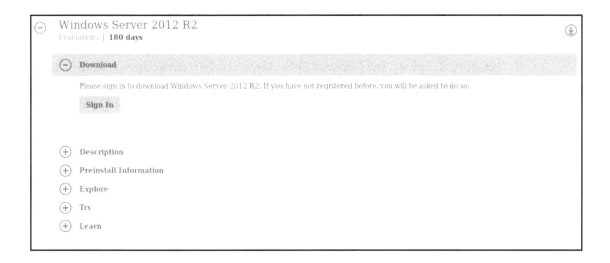

Sign up, login, and download Mircrosoft Windows Server 2012r2

Download the ISO from a workstation on the same physical network as your Proxmox VE server, and then upload the image to PVE via the web interface as described in the preceding section.

When the upload is complete, it should be visible in the **Content** tab of the local storage.

Viewing available image files

Configuring and creating the virtual machine

To configure and create a Windows Server VM quickly, follow these steps:

1. To get started, upload the Microsoft Windows Server from your workstation to the Proxmox VE server as described previously.

2. With the OS install media now available to PVE, we can click on the **Create VM** button to initiate the **Create:** Virtual Machine dialog as described previously. Complete the fields in the **General** tab, as illustrated in the following screenshot:

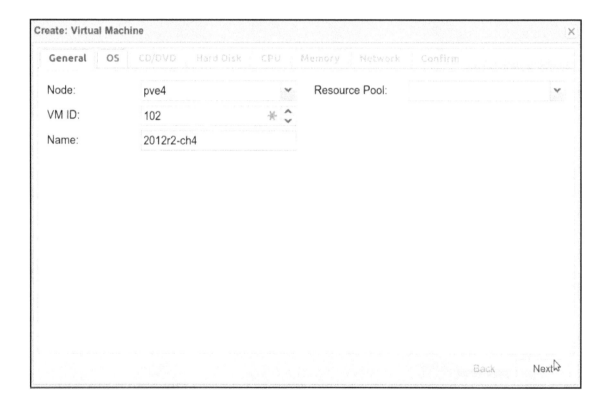

3. Proceed to the **OS** tab of the dialog by clicking on **Next**. The left column of this dialog consists of options for Microsoft operating systems. Choose the top-most option, **Microsoft Windows 8/Server 2012**, and click on **Next** to continue to the **CD/DVD** tab.

Create: Virtual Machine   ×

| General | OS | CD/DVD | Hard Disk | CPU | Memory | Network | Confirm |

Microsoft Windows   Linux/Other OS types

- ○ Microsoft Windows 8/10/2012 (win8)   ○ Linux 4.X/3.X/2.6 Kernel (l26)
- ○ Microsoft Windows 7/2008r2 (win7)   ○ Linux 2.4 Kernel (l24)
- ○ Microsoft Windows Vista/2008 (w2k8)   ○ Solaris Kernel (solaris)
- ○ Microsoft Windows XP/2003 (wxp)   ○ Other OS types (other)
- ○ Microsoft Windows 2000 (w2k)

                                                              Back   Next

---

4. On the **CD/DVD** tab, select the top option to choose an ISO file. With the **Storage** field set to local, use the drop-down menu for the **ISO Image** field to choose the uploaded 2012r2 image. Click on **Next** to continue.

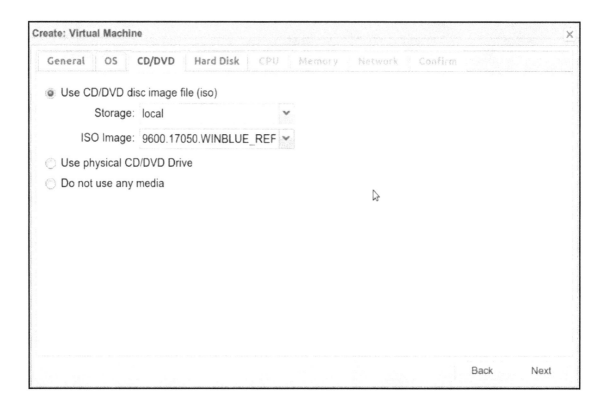

5. On the **Hard Disk** tab, stay mindful that Server 2012r2 requires at least 32 GB of storage. Set an appropriate disk size and ensure that **Bus/Device** is set to **IDE**; avoid choosing **virtio**. Set the format to **QEMU image format (qcow2)** and click on **Next** to continue to the **CPU** tab.

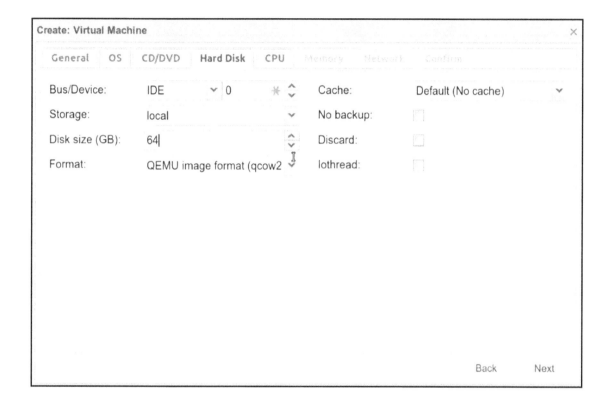

We'll cover **Bus/Device** types in the next chapter.

6. On the **CPU** tab, configure the number of sockets and the number of cores per socket to commit to the VM. For the purposes of this exercise, I've set **Sockets** to 1 and set the number of cores to 2. The **Type** field should be set to **Default (kvm64)**. Keep in mind that we can change the CPU configuration later as necessary. Click on **Next** to configure the memory for the VM.

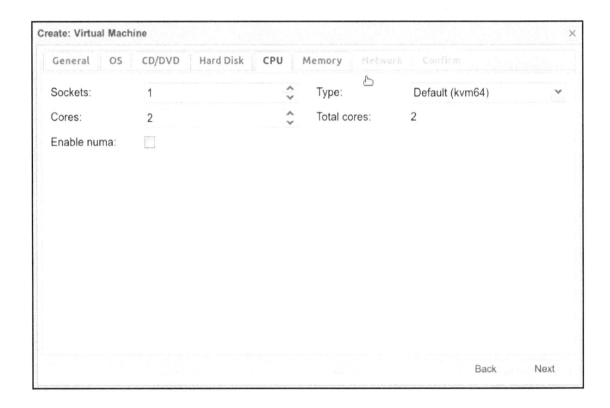

7. Windows Server 2012r2 requires a minimum of 512 MB of RAM. As illustrated in the following screenshot, PVE provides an option for using a fixed amount of RAM or automatically allocating RAM within a specified range.

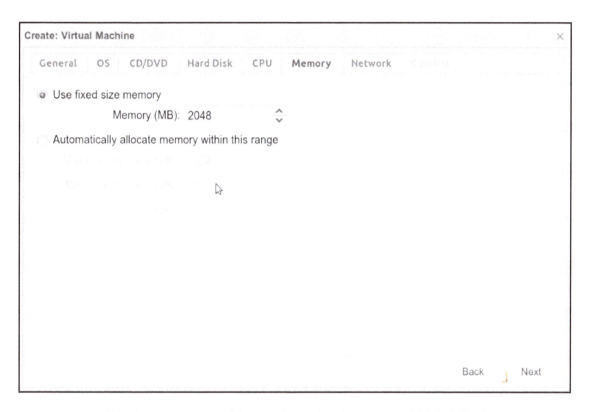

For the purposes of this exercise, a fixed amount of 2,048 MB of memory has been allocated, with the understanding that this can be easily changed later. When the memory is tuned the way you'd like, click on **Next** to configure the network.

8. As the following screenshot illustrates, the IP address of a VM can't be preconfigured like it can be with containers:

As illustrated, **Bridged mode** is selected rather than **NAT mode**. This choice is deliberate. In this case, **NAT mode** would prevent us from accessing the virtual machine's desktop through Microsoft's, Remote Desktop Protocol or Remote Server Administration Tool.

Bridged mode provides more choices for accessing the VM, since it's somewhat analogous to attaching a machine to a switch on the physical network. There are consequences for this decision in regard to isolation and security, especially with Proxmox's firewall disabled.

 To learn more about PVE's integrated firewall features, visit `https://pve .proxmox.com/wiki/Proxmox_VE_Firewall#Enabling_firewall_f or_qemu_guest_and_openvz_veth`.

Networking can be reconfigured at any point after the creation of the virtual machine.

When the **Network** tab is configured to your satisfaction, click on **Next** to view a configuration summary and to confirm the configuration.

9. The final tab, labeled **Confirm**, provides a summary of the VM's configuration and the opportunity to finally create the VM.

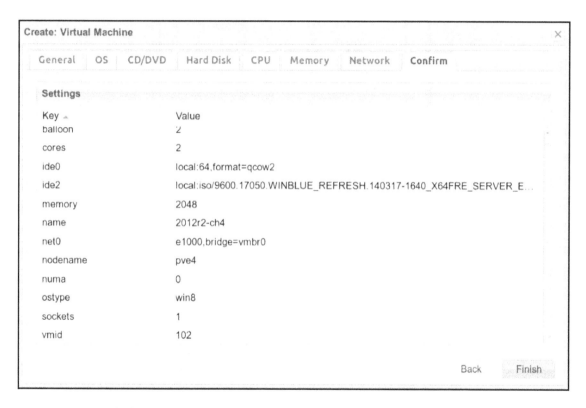

Click on the **Finish** button to confirm your configuration and create the virtual machine, but feel encouraged to use this opportunity to return to a prior step and adjust the configuration.

Keep in mind, however, that many of these settings can be changed even after the VM is created and the OS installed, sometimes without even rebooting the machine.

Within 30 seconds, the new VM will appear in the left frame of the Web interface:

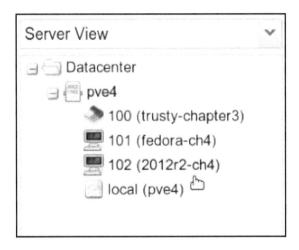

There's another way

Note that in this chapter, the Windows Server VM is configured so we can quickly try Windows Server virtualization using a TechNet trial; the configuration is not optimized for performance and is not ideal for production. Ideally, a Windows Server virtual machine in Proxmox VE that is production ready will be configured to take advantage of paravirtualization; in PVE, this is just a matter of choosing **virtio** on two tabs. On the **Hard Disk** tab, consider choosing **virtio** instead of **IDE**; and on the **Network** tab, consider virtio rather than Intel E1000. This does, however, complicate the Windows Server installation since it doesn't ship with virtio drivers. Consequently, we'd need to upload drivers on an ISO image to PVE and make them available to Windows Server early in the OS installation process. Fortunately, this configuration is well documented on the PVE wiki at `https://pve.proxmox.com/wiki/Windows_2012_gue st_best_practices`.

Downloading the example code

You can download the example code files for this book from your account at `http://www.packtpub.com`. If you purchased this book elsewhere, you can visit `http://www.packtpub.com/support` and register to have the files e-mailed directly to you.

You can download the code files by following these steps:

1. Log in or register to our website using your e-mail address and password.
2. Hover the mouse pointer on the **SUPPORT** tab at the top.
3. Click on **Code Downloads & Errata**.
4. Enter the name of the book in the **Search** box.
5. Select the book for which you're looking to download the code files.
6. Choose from the drop-down menu where you purchased this book from.
7. Click on **Code Download**.

Once the file is downloaded, please make sure that you unzip or extract the folder using the latest version of:

- WinRAR / 7-Zip for Windows
- Zipeg / iZip / UnRarX for Mac
- 7-Zip / PeaZip for Linux

Starting the VM and installing Windows Server

After the virtual machine is configured and available for use, select it in the **Server View** in the upper left pane of the web interface. Starting the VM is as simple as pressing the Start button that is revealed in the right pane as previously described.

When the machine is started, its icon will change from a monitor with a black screen to one with a white screen.

To access the machine's display via noVNC, click on the **Console** button; a window will popup that allows you to watch the VM's boot from the Windows Server 2012r2 install disc and will eventually display the **Windows Setup** wizard:

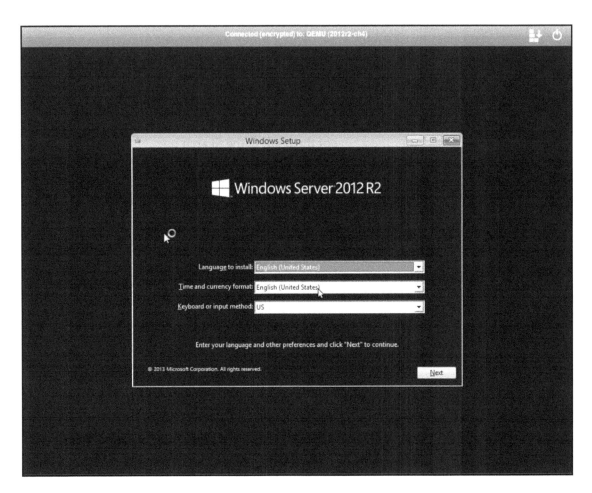

Follow the on-screen instructions to complete the installation and configuration of Windows Server 2012r2.

Support for installation of this OS is available at `https://technet.micr osoft.com/en-us/library/jj134246.aspx`.

Once the Windows Setup dialogs are complete, the installation will proceed and the machine will restart a few times until it is ready for a user to log in. Log in to the server to see the new desktop.

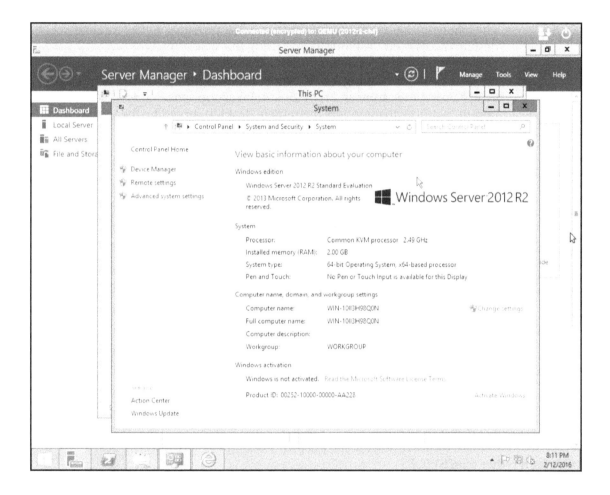

Note that both the two preceding screenshots have double mouse-pointers. One for the local workstation and one for the desktop accessed via noVNC. This is awkward and cumbersome.

noVNC
The name noVNC is counterintuitive; noVNC provides, in fact, remote desktop access and desktop sharing using the VNC protocol. However, noVNC does distinguish itself; instead of connecting to a remote computer running a VNC server by configuring a client, choosing noVNC produces, from an HTML5- and JavaScript-enabled browser, a pop-up window that renders the remote desktop served by the virtual machine.

There's a simple solution, enable **Use tablet for pointer** in the VM's **Options** tab if it's not already enabled:

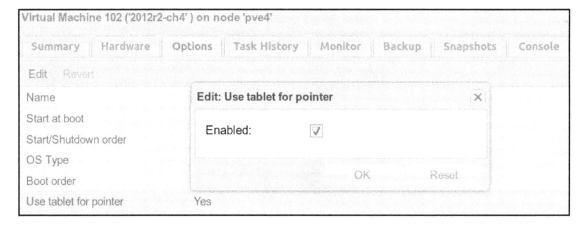

If that doesn't resolve the issue, ensure the **Display** field on the hardware tab is set to **Default** rather than **SPICE**.

Creating a VM for Fedora 23 Server

In the previous sections, we detailed the configuration of a virtual machine intended for use with Windows Server 2012r2. In this section, we'll build on our experience and apply what we learned to building a server running Fedora 23 (Server). Creating this VM offers a simple way to practice using paravirtualization for the virtual network interface card and the virtual hard-disk interface.

1. Review Fedora 23 Server installation at `http://www.tecmint.com/installat ion-of-fedora-23-server-and-administration-with-cockpit-tool/`.

2. Download the netinst ISO from `http://mirrors.rit.edu/fedora/fedora/l inux/releases/23/Server/x86_64/iso/Fedora-Server-netinst-x86_64 -23.iso`.

Index of /fedora/fedora/linux/releases/23/Server /x86_64/iso/

Name	Last Modified	Size	Type
Parent Directory/		-	Directory
Fedora-Server-23-x86_64-CHECKSUM	2015-Oct-30 16:37:19	1.1K	application/octet-stream
Fedora-Server-DVD-x86_64-23.iso	2015-Oct-29 21:50:17	2.0G	application/octet-stream
Fedora-Server-netinst-x86_64-23.iso	2015-Oct-29 21:48:25	415.0M	application/octet-stream

lighttpd Mirror info at `http://mirrors.rit.edu/`

Downloading the Fedora 23 net installation image

3. Login to the PVE web interface.
4. Upload the image to PVE's local storage as previously described.
5. Click on **Create VM**, just as we did for Windows Server 2012r2.

6. In the **General** tab of the **Create: Virtual Machine** dialog, give the machine a well-considered name; in the following screenshot, `fedora-ch4` is used and the VM is assigned VM ID 101. Proceed to the **OS** tab.

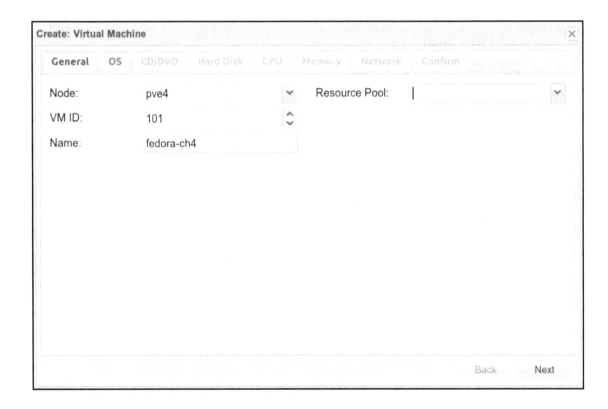

7. On the **OS** tab, there are four options that aren't for Microsoft Windows; for Fedora 23, choose the **Linux 4.X/3.X/2.6 Kernel (I26)** radio button and proceed to the **CD/DVD** tab.

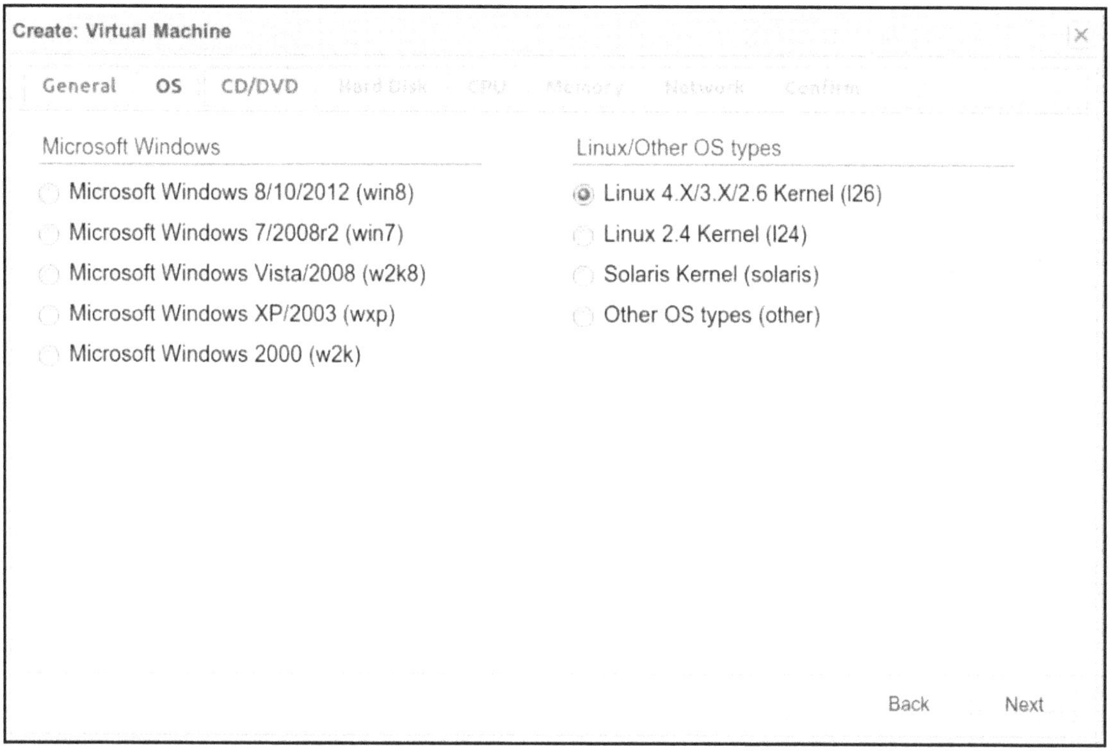

Create: Virtual Machine   ☒

General   **OS**   CD/DVD   Hard Disk   CPU   Memory   Network   Confirm

Microsoft Windows   Linux/Other OS types

○ Microsoft Windows 8/10/2012 (win8)   ◉ Linux 4.X/3.X/2.6 Kernel (I26)

○ Microsoft Windows 7/2008r2 (win7)   ○ Linux 2.4 Kernel (I24)

○ Microsoft Windows Vista/2008 (w2k8)   ○ Solaris Kernel (solaris)

○ Microsoft Windows XP/2003 (wxp)   ○ Other OS types (other)

○ Microsoft Windows 2000 (w2k)

                                                          Back   Next

---

8. Choose the first option on the **CD/DVD** tab, the **Use CD/DVD disc image file (iso)** radio button; choose **local** in the **Storage** field and choose the image file uploaded in step 4 from the **ISO Image** drop-down menu:

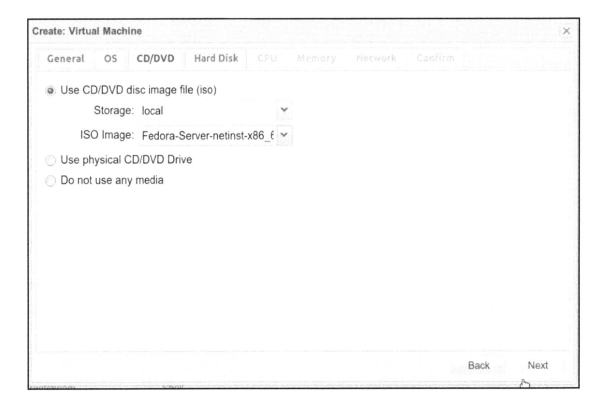

Selecting the Fedora install disk on the CD/DVD tab

Proceed to the **Hard Disk** tab to configure a virtual hard disk for the Fedora Server VM.

9. On this virtual machine, we'll rely on paravirtualization for improved efficiency. On the **Hard Disk** tab, choose **VIRTIO** from the **Bus/Device** drop-down menu. Note that in the following screenshot, the **Disk size** field has changed from the default 32 GB to 64 GB; please choose a disk size at your discretion. When finished, continue to the **CPU** tab.

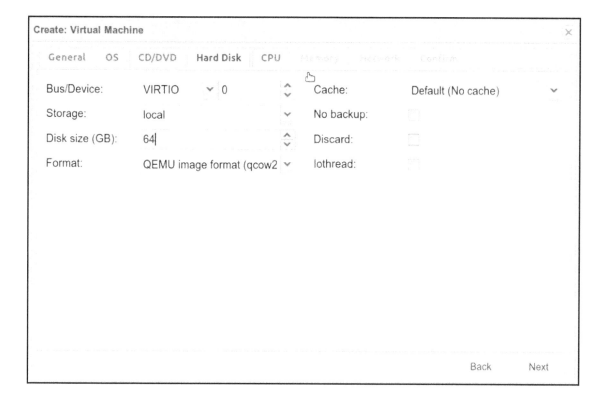

Configuring the Virtual Disk

10. We'll configure the **CPU** tab just as we did for the Windows Server 2012r2 VM we created in the preceding section: allocate 1 socket and 2 cores, and specify **Default (KVM64)** in the **Type** drop-down menu. When the **CPU** tab is configured to your satisfaction, proceed to the Memory tab to allocate RAM for the VM.

11. Use your discretion on the **Memory** tab. In the screenshot below, a fixed-size memory of 1024 MB is specified. Once you've allocated RAM according to your preferences, continue to the **Network** tab.

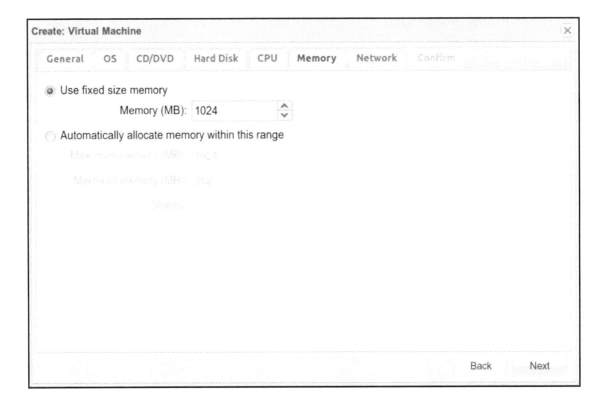

Allocate RAM for the Fedora virtual machine on the Memory tab

12. On the network tab, let's configure Fedora so it's accessible to other machines on the physical network; just as we did with Microsoft Server, choose the **Bridged mode** radio button. If your PVE host has a single network interface, set the **Bridge** drop-down menu to vmbr0; otherwise, use your discretion to choose an appropriate bridge.

Then, in the right-hand column of the **Network** tab, select **VirtIO (paravirtualized)** as the **Model** of the virtual network interface. To review, **Intel E1000** is our most widely compatible choice, while **virtio** is the best-performing alternative; both are supported "out of the box" by Fedora Server.

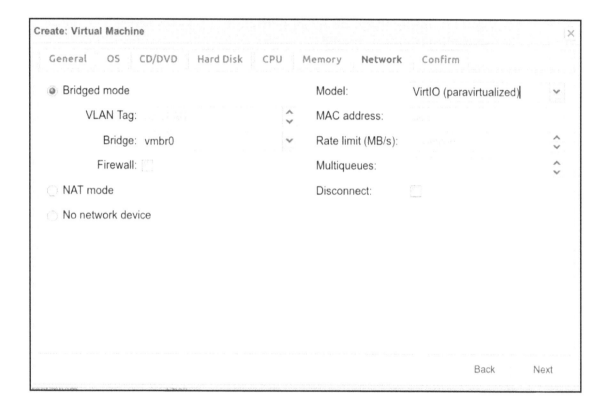

Configuring bridged mode network on the Network tab

Proceed to the **Confirm** tab and commit to the VM configuration; this is a good opportunity to make discretionary changes to the configuration before building the VM.

Keep in mind through this process that, in every case except that of the virtual hard disk, the resources allocated here can be changed later with minimal fuss.

13. Click on **Finish** to create the virtual machine and close the **Create: Virtual Machine** dialog.

> We used the default display option in the Windows Server machine we configured in the previous section. It's a great option that works with an established technology underlying PVE's noVNC console.
>
> However, by installing additional software on Windows Server, we could have relied on SPICE instead.

SPICE
This option appears in the menu as **SPICE** (the Simple Protocol for Independent Computing Environments), but it refers either to the SPICE protocol that's relied on, or to the dependence on a combination of SPICE components, including guest tools (installed on the VM) and the SPICE client installed on the Workstation. We can infer from this that making use of SPICE requires some post-installation work. SPICE is the only solution whose explicit mission is to provide remote access to VMs. Moreover, clients are available for mobile devices and several operating systems, and the protocol offers many options for both implementation and usage. Red Hat is the current developer of this open source solution, and it promotes it heavily as part of its KVM-QEMU virtualization platform. The spice-module is also, however, integrated into Proxmox VE for use with its own KVM-QEMU VMs. Since Fedora Server includes software to support the SPICE display, let's see what preparing for that is like.

14. While the Fedora Server virtual machine is still stopped, select its **Hardware** tab.

15. Double-click on the **Display** configuration; the **Edit: Display** dialog opens, with a drop-down menu labeled **Graphic Card**. Change the selection from **Default** to **SPICE** and click on the **OK** button:

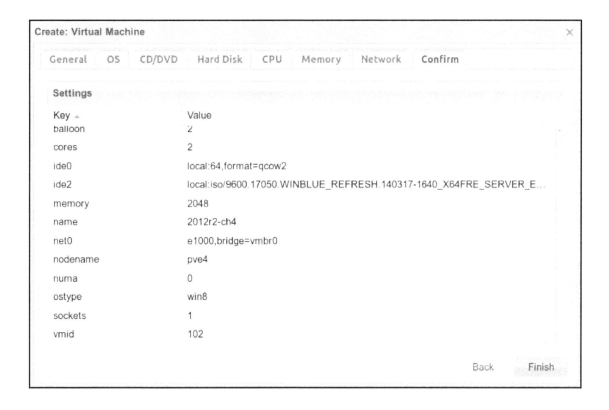

Configuring the VM for use with the SPICE console

When you're ready to install Fedora 23 Server, select the VM in the left pane of the browser window.

16. Once selected, start the VM. Click on the arrow beside the console button to reveal a choice between the noVNC and SPICE consoles.

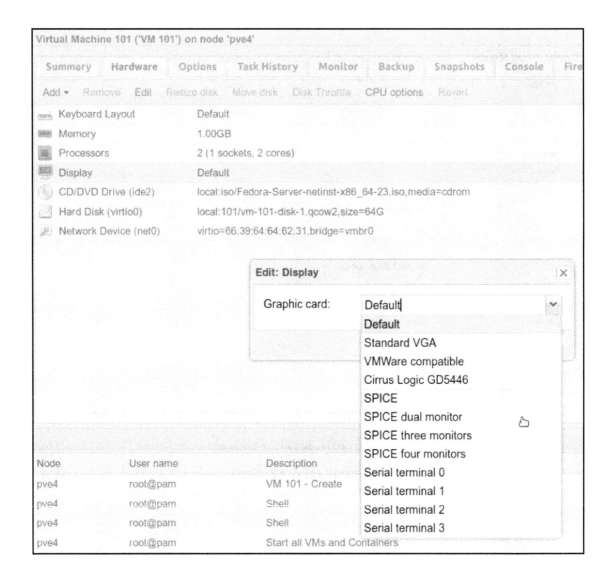

Choosing the SPICE console to access a running virtual machine

17. Select **SPICE** to launch a popup console browser window.

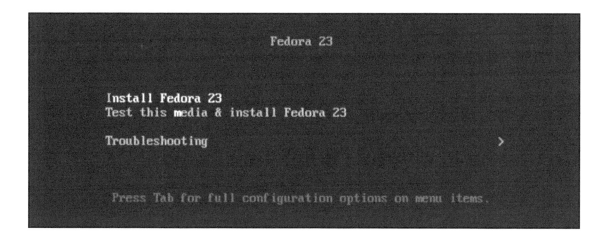

Initiating the installation of Fedora 23 on the virtual machine with the SPICE console

Proceed with the installation by pressing *i* or navigating to **Install Fedora 23** with the up and down cursor keys on the keyboard.

After about 20 seconds, the graphical installer for Fedora 23 will begin to ask configuration questions, starting with the language to use with the installer, and moving on to the network configuration and host name. Ultimately, you'll also be asked to set the password of the root user and create additional accounts.

 If you have questions about network configuration for your new Fedora 23 VM, see the *Fedora 23 Networking Guide* at `https://docs.fedoraprojec t.org/en-US/Fedora/23/pdf/Networking_Guide/Fedora-23-Netw orking_Guide-en-US.pdf`.

Follow the onscreen instructions to complete the Fedora 23 installation. The time spent on installation is contingent on how you allocated resources, how fast your Internet connection is, and what packages you choose to install during the initial Fedora 23 configuration process.

Support for Fedora 23 Server installation

Fedora 23 Server features can be found at `https://getfedora.org/en/server/`.

The official Fedora 23 Server installation guide is at `https://docs.fedoraproject.org/en-US/Fedora/23/html/Installation_Guide/`.

For post installation suggestions, go to `http://www.tecmint.com/things-to-do-after-fedora-23-installation/`.

Command line virtual machine creation

We can use the `qm create` command to create a Proxmox VE virtual machine from the command line. This is a boon to command line users and those looking to script automated solutions.

The bash script that follows creates a VM to run Fedora 23 Server:

```
#!/bin/bash -ex
# Creates a VM intended for Fedora 23 Server
 qm create 103 \
     -balloon 512 \
     -bootdisk virtio0 \
     -cores 2 \
     -ide2 local:iso/Fedora-Server-netinst-x86_64-23.iso,media=cdrom \
     -memory 1024 \
     -name fedora-server-ch4 \
     -net0 virtio,bridge=vmbr0 \
     -numa 0 \
     -ostype l26 \
     -sockets 1 \
     -virtio0 local:101/vm-101-disk-1.qcow2,size=32G \
     -vga qxl
```

See `https://pve.proxmox.com/wiki/Manual:_qm` to learn more about creating virtual machines from the Proxmox VE command line interface.

Summary

To the shrewd administrator, the capability to utilize containers in conjunction with virtual machines in production environments offers flexibility and increased opportunities for professional discretion and informed choices. System virtualization continues to have a currency in the datacenter.

Consequently, we began this chapter with a high-level overview of the VM creation and configuration process with Proxmox VE—from obtaining the install media, to configuring the VM, and installing the operating system.

Afterwards, we took that abstract outline and applied it to two concrete cases: the creation of a Microsoft Windows Server 2012r2 and Fedora 23 Server virtual machines.

In Chapter 5, *Working with Virtual Drives*, you will learn all you need to know to make informed choices when determining what format best suits our virtual hard drives.

We'll give particular attention to making use of VMs created with Oracle's VirtualBox, VMware Player, and VMware workstation in our new Proxmox virtual environments.

There's a certain satisfaction in repurposing something that was never intended for our scenario.

Let's experience that thrill next.

5
Working with Virtual Disks

Chapter 4, *Creating a Virtual Machine*, introduced the creation of virtual machines using the Proxmox VE management interface as well as the command line. After an outline of common steps in the procedure, we quickly glossed over creating two virtual machines with two network operating systems: **Windows Server 2012r2** and **Fedora 23 Server**.

Our most fundamental goal with this chapter is to empower ourselves to make more informed and fully-deliberated decisions affecting the efficiency and reliability of a Proxmox VE virtual machine guest based on its specific use case.

We will accomplish this goal by achieving the following concrete objectives:

- Choose deliberately from among virtual disk image formats available for use through the Proxmox VE interface
- Choose an appropriate bus/interface by which a virtual disk will connect to a guest
- Choose an appropriate cache setting for our use cases

In this chapter, then, we elaborate on one critical, and potentially the most valuable, virtual machine component: the **virtual disk** that provides **secondary storage**.

We will then revisit the virtual machine creation process to elaborate on specific options glossed over in Chapter 4, *Creating a Virtual Machine*:

- Choosing a virtual disk format
- Choosing an interface
- Selecting a cache option

Understanding virtual disks

This section focuses first on the terms we should be familiar with to build on our understanding of virtual disks.

After we've agreed on terms, we'll explore virtual disk configuration options that we saw in `Chapter 4`, *Creating a Virtual Machine*, but did not explore: virtual disk image formats, bus/interface options, and disk **cache** options.

Coming to terms

Secondary storage is as integral to virtual machines as it is to physical computers. While **hard disk drives** (HDDs) are hardly the most expensive hardware in PCs, we could compellingly argue that they are the most valuable, so far as we rely on them to store and provide access to our data, often the unique fruit of our hard labor.

Throughout this chapter, the term Virtual Disk will refer to a file or set of files that, to a virtual machine, represent a hard disk drive and behave just as a physical hard disk drive or **solid-state drive** (SSD) does for a physical computer.

The similarities between a physical hard disk drive and a virtual disk are, as you might expect, as follows:

- Identical file system options
- The same strong understanding of partitions and partition tables is required of administrators with fluency in using the same partition editing tools we'd use on physical machines
- Identical formatting procedures and options
- The same support for LVM

However, the striking differences must be made explicit. A physical hard disk drive unit includes more than just the media that stores data.

The media component of HDDs is constituted by a stack of double-sided, physical platters rotating around a common spindle within a vacuum-sealed structure.

Also within the vacuum seal is the physical, mechanical apparatus that reads and writes data on the platters. It includes an armature that moves read/write heads to specific locations on the platters.

A virtual disk has a storage capacity and can be written to or read from like a hard disk; however, the media is simply a file or series of files on the host that uses one of three disk image formats compatible with Proxmox VE: **QCOW2**, **RAW**, and **VMDK**.

> A fourth option is available when using iSCSI shared storage: RAW as LVM partitions. In this section, we'll address only RAW, qcow2, and VMDK images.

As you'll learn later, each of the three virtual disk image formats explicitly supported by the Proxmox VE management interface provides slightly different advantages and disadvantages. For us, this provides extended flexibility.

For example, in addition to the backup methods an administrator would use to ensure the safety and integrity of the host and the guest data, it can be a simple matter to make backups or snapshots of the state of one or more virtual machines. Restoring an image to a previous state is simple too.

Another difference between the virtual disk and a hard disk drive is that the bus, the interface between the motherboard and the disk, is physically incorporated into a hard disk unit.

This is handled quite differently on a Proxmox VE virtual machine, on which you choose the type of bus that's used to communicate with the virtual disk based on your preferences for the specific virtual machine.

The bus, then, isn't at all part of the virtual disk image; instead, it's part of the virtual machine configuration. On Proxmox VE, there are bus choices available through a simple drop-down box.

Another subcomponent of the physical hard disk drive that is not represented in a virtual disk is the cache subsystem (or, more accurately, *disk buffer*). The cache, designed to speed up the retrieval of data, constitutes, like the bus interface, a part of a virtual machine's configuration, rather than part of the virtual disk.

Visualizing a hard disk with a SATA interface and disk buffer on the control board

In this section, we determined that *virtual disk* will be used to describe the file or group of files that serve as virtual machines' secondary storage devices. In addition, we articulated similarities between physical drives and virtual drives. We then contrasted the physical components of a hard disk drive and how virtualization with Proxmox VE abstracts these components.

Proxmox VE's configuration process completely divorces the storage media from both the bus and the disk cache or disk buffer, which again frees us to make more deliberate choices about which combination of virtual disk image format, bus, and cache to choose.

The remaining subsections articulate the features of each image format, bus option, and disk cache option available to us through Proxmox VE.

Understanding virtual disk configuration

Recall from Chapter 4, *Creating a Virtual Machine* that we created new virtual machines from the Proxmox VE interface by clicking on the **Create VM** button toward the top of the page and running through the new VM's configuration options.

Regarding the fourth tab in the configuration dialog, **Hard Disk**, Chapter 4, *Creating a Virtual Machine* restricted its concern to defining the size of the virtual disk.

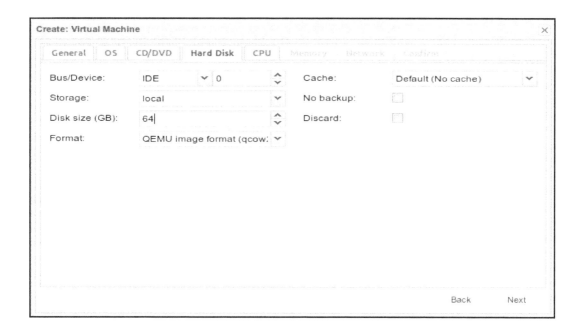

The Hard Disk tab in the Create: Virtual Machine dialog

In this section, we elaborate on three additional characteristics that can be defined through the **Hard Disk** tab:

- Virtual disk format
- Bus/Device (interface)
- Cache (disk buffer)

With at least three configuration options available for each, let's explore how your choices can affect performance and features.

Choosing a virtual disk format

According to *Mastering Proxmox*, Proxmox VE's preferred image format for virtual disks is RAW. However, it also supports KVM's `qcow2` format and VMDK images commonly associated with VMware products.

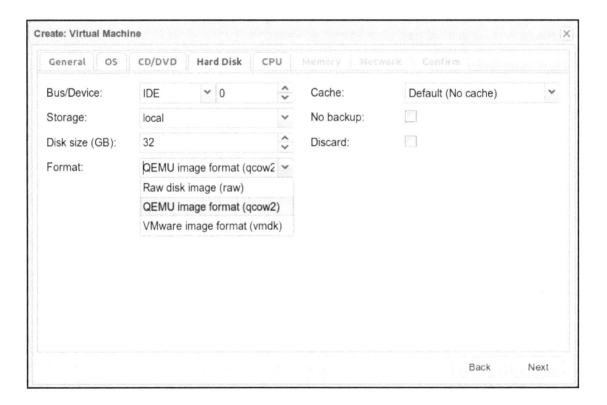

To learn more about image formats and their manipulation, visit `https:/ /en.wikibooks.org/wiki/QEMU/Images`.

QCOW2

QCOW2 is the second release of QEMU's copy-on-write image format. Since Proxmox VE relies on KVM-QEMU for its virtual machine features, QCOW2 is its native and default format.

As its name suggests, this format supports **copy on write**. This feature allows the VM to store changes made to a base image in a separate QCOW2 file. The metadata (data about data) of the new QCOW2 file includes, for example, the path to the base image.

When the VM seeks to retrieve data, it checks first to see whether the specific data can be retrieved from the new image; if it is not in the new image, the data is retrieved from the base image referred to by the metadata.

To learn more about the QCOW2 image structure, visit `https://people.gnome.org/~markmc/qcow-image-format.html`.

QCOW2 images also grow as needed (**thin provisioning**), a feature that distinguishes them from RAW images, for which all the space requested at their creation is immediately allocated to a file (**thick provisioning**).

Consequently, QCOW2 images will be smaller than RAW images in almost any case even when the host's file system doesn't support sparse files. However, the RAW image will have better throughput since it doesn't have to grow as data is written and because it doesn't depend on an intermediary software layer.

We should take note however, that if PVE has plenty of fast RAM and runs on a recent SSD drive instead of a hard drive, the difference in throughput between a RAW image and a QCOW2 image is much less visible. As we continue to explore image types, keep in mind the impact newer hardware, with ever-decreasing prices, can have on performance.

A sparse file is one that attempts to use file system space more efficiently when the file itself is mostly empty. This is achieved by writing metadata representing the empty blocks to disk, rather than the actual empty space which makes up the block. Consequently, less disk space is used. Only when the block contains real data is the full block size written to disk as its literal size (`https://en.wikipedia.org/wiki/Sparse_file`).
For a list of file systems with support for sparse files, visit `https://en.wikipedia.org/wiki/Comparison_of_file_systems#Allocation_and_layout_policies`.

QCOW2's snapshot and temporary snapshot support allows an image to contain multiple snapshots from prior moments in the image's history.

Temporary snapshots store changes until the VM powers off, at which point the snapshot is discarded. Standard snapshots, in contrast, allow us to return to prior states in an image's history.

 To learn more about QCOW2 snapshots with Proxmox VE, visit their wiki page at `https://pve.proxmox.com/wiki/Live_Snapshots`. For more about the mechanics behind QCOW2's snapshot support, visit `https://kashyapc.fedorapeople.org/virt/lc-2012/snapshots-handout.html`.

RAW

RAW and QCOW2 are the two most supported Proxmox VE formats discussed in Proxmox VE forums.

Compared to both QCOW2 and VMDK images, RAW virtual disks are quite simple; and unlike the other formats supported by Proxmox VE, RAW doesn't rely on an intermediary software layer.

Consequently, RAW is a more efficient option and should be given all due consideration when the performance of a virtual machine is of supreme importance — particularly RAW on LVM.

Moreover, RAW images can be directly and simply mounted on the Proxmox VE host for direct manipulation without requiring access through the guest.

 Mounting a RAW file
To walk through this procedure, consider visiting `http://equivocation.org/node/107` or `http://forensicswiki.org/wiki/Mounting_Disk_Images#To_mount_a_disk_image_on_Linux`; both pages recommend using the `kpartx` utility, available in the default Debian repositories.

However, unlike QCOW2 images, RAW images are not feature rich; there's no inherent support for snapshots, no thin provisioning, and so on. They are composed of raw data, built sector by sector until they reach their fixed capacity.

Performance, then, is the real boon of RAW images as virtual drives; if you're relying on a hard disk drive rather than a solid state drive, and reliable, snappy performance is critical, as it might be for a database server, for example, then choose RAW and forego the rich feature set offered by QCOW2.

Although pre-allocating storage for accumulating VM guests can be an unnecessary strain on resources, keep in mind that RAW virtual drives too can be resized.

As is the case with QCOW2, only part of the resizing process can be accomplished through the management interface Proxmox VE provides.

 The process for resizing both RAW and QCOW2 images is documented on the Proxmox VE wiki page at `https://pve.proxmox.com/wiki/Resiz ing_disks#Enlarge_the_virtual_disk.28s.29_in_Proxmox`.

VMDK

Virtual machine disk (**VMDK**) is the preferred virtual disk format for VMware virtualization products. Having said that, the format was subsequently opened up to other developers and vendors, and has become a popular virtual disk format to support.

While KVM-QEMU currently supports versions 3, 4, and 6 of the format, and Proxmox VE can create VMs with VMDK images, it's recommended that PVE users rely on QEMU native formats—QCOW2 and RAW—whenever circumstances allow.

Realistically, however, circumstances aren't always ideal; so before we address bus types, let's touch on a few relevant points regarding VMDK virtual disks.

Like QCOW2, VMDK is a complex format with a rich feature set (in fact, it has four sub-formats).

For example, the VMDK format supports thin and thick provisioning. Thin VMDK images, like their QCOW2 counterparts, are slower than preallocated, or thick-provisioned, VMDK images. As we'd expect, they are significantly smaller.

Likewise, both VMDK and QCOW2 formats support multiple snapshots that enable administrators to restore a virtual machine to a prior state.

While the format's feature set is rich, not all its features are supported by the Proxmox VE interface, even when the underlying virtualization layer can handle them.

For example, the VMDK format includes a subformat that splits a virtual disk into 2 GB chunks, essentially to support mobility. This subformat isn't supported by Proxmox VE.

While Proxmox VE does invite us to create virtual machines with VMDK images, rely as much as possible on QCOW2 and RAW virtual disk formats:

- Assuming your PVE is built around a traditional hard disk drive, RAW is ideal for database applications, for example, because it has the performance advantage.
- QCOW2 offers an extremely powerful feature set that could come at the cost of performance if you're not relying on SSD storage. In addition, QCOW2 is more conservative in its use of hardware resources.

If you've inherited a virtual disk in the VMDK format, it can be converted to either the QCOW2 or RAW format using the `qemu-img` command.

On the other hand, if you're creating a Proxmox VE , reliance on the VMDK format should be reserved for very deliberate and purposeful edge cases.

Full documentation for the `qemu-img` command is available on the Web at `https://www.suse.com/documentation/sles11/book_kvm/data/cha_qemu_guest_inst_qemu-img.html` (SUSE) and `https://docs.fedoraproject.org/en-US/Fedora/18/html/Virtualization_Administration_Guide/sect-Virtualization-Tips_and_tricks-Using_qemu_img.html` (Fedora).
The sparse but comprehensive GNU/Linux main page is available at `http://linux.die.net/man/1/qemu-img`.

Choosing a bus

Along with **Format** options, the **Hard Disk** tab of the **Create: Virtual Machine** dialog offers a drop-down menu for the **Bus/Device** with which to interface the virtual disk.

As illustrated here, four options are available:

- **IDE**
- **SATA**
- **VIRTIO**
- **SCSI**

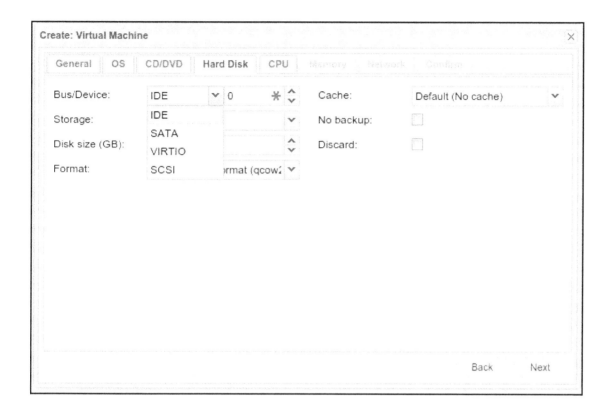

Bus/Device options

 Note that with the exception of I/O performance, the characteristics of the virtual SATA, IDE, and SCSI buses will be the same as their physical counterparts. For details about each, visit Wikipedia:
SATA: https://en.wikipedia.org/wiki/Serial_ATA
IDE/PATA: https://en.wikipedia.org/wiki/Parallel_ATA
SCSI: https://en.wikipedia.org/wiki/SCSI

Of the four options, two are provided as convenient support for compatibility with legacy systems: **IDE** and **SCSI**. (IDE is thus the dialog's default option.)

The **SATA** option has more currency, and behaves as one would expect a SATA interface to behave — with one significant exception: the **SATA** option does not provide a performance boost over **IDE**, for example.

I/O performance, in this case, is determined almost entirely by the host's hardware configuration. The VM will not be able to read and write faster than the physical hardware permits.

Since the limits of the host's hardware I/O performance can't be overcome, KVM-QEMU addresses, instead, the overhead attached to the virtualization process, the other factor affecting performance in this case.

KVM-QEMU provides a paravirtualization solution called **virtio** that allows the guest and hypervisor to work more cooperatively and efficiently with one another without the virtualization overhead.

Paravirtualization refers to software components that are aware they are running in a VM. Virtio drivers for use with KVM-QEMU VMs communicate directly with the Proxmox VE host in our case. Typical of paravirtualized drivers, virtio drivers are optimized to share queues, buffers, and other data with Proxmox VE to improve throughput and to reduce latency (vTerminology: A Guide to Key Virtualization Terminology is available at `http://www.globalknowledge.com`). We'll return to virtio drivers again in the context of network interfaces in `Chapter 6`, *Networking with Proxmox VE*.

This solution, **VIRTIO**, is the only **Bus/Device** option that affects the I/O performance of the VM.

The ability to take advantage of a guest's virtio devices requires that drivers are available for the guest's OS. As the Proxmox VE wiki page points out, recent Linux kernels already include the virtio drivers; therefore, any recent GNU/Linux distribution running on a Proxmox VE VM "should recognize virtio devices exposed by the KVM hypervisor" (`https://pve.proxmox.com/wiki/Windows_VirtIO_Drivers`).

VM guests running GNU/Linux, therefore, do not require any additional explicit configuration steps.

VM guests running a Microsoft Windows OS will need signed drivers installed before the virtio device will be recognized. As you may suspect, there's a hitch here, since the OS install process needs the device driver in order to recognize and install to the virtual disk.

We can employ any of several tactics to overcome this problem.

For additional information on Microsoft operating systems and virtio devices, visit `https://pve.proxmox.com/wiki/Windows_VirtIO_Dri vers`.

This subsection puts a significant and just emphasis on the performance increase virtio paravirtualization supported by KVM-QEMU provides.

To summarize, the only time we shouldn't use virtio paravirtualization is when the required drivers aren't available for the OS intended for the virtual machine. Because it will significantly improve I/O throughput and alleviate some of the overhead associated with full virtualization, we should rely on virtio whenever it is a realistic alternative.

However, let's keep in mind that IDE and SCSI are also viable bus alternatives, but provided primarily for legacy devices and to serve the interests of compatibility and flexibility. SATA, however, has significant currency at this point, so it's a viable alternative if circumstances just don't allow you to take advantage of the virtio solution.

 There is another case when virtio paravirtualization is not viable: when a VM has been converted from a physical machine and one thus needs to install the drivers before rebooting to rely on virtio.

The next subsection focuses on the five disk caching/buffering options available for our Proxmox VE virtual machines.

Understanding cache options

The **Hard Disk** tab of the **Create: Virtual Machine** dialog includes a field labeled **Cache** that accepts five distinct values:

- **Default (No cache)**
- **Direct sync**
- **Write through**
- **Write back**
- **Write back (unsafe)**

Essentially, the chosen setting determines how the abstraction of a HDD's buffer should be handled. With Proxmox VE, the choice of cache has been demonstrated to significantly affect I/O performance.

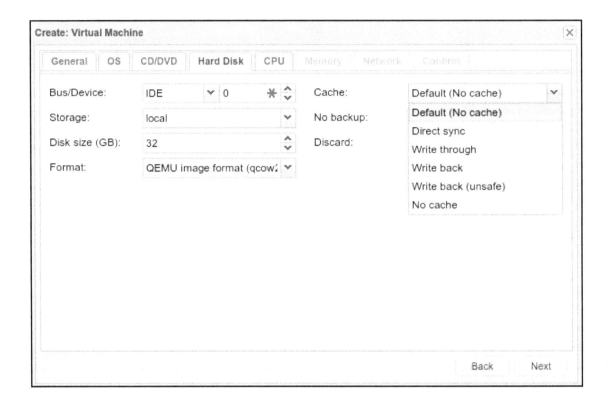

Proxmox VE cache options

After working to somewhat articulate the function of a disk buffer, this section will briefly explore recommendations to optimize the performance of a VM.

On a physical hard disk, the disk buffer is a kind of memory on the controller board mounted outside the vacuum-sealed disk housing. Contemporary hard-disk drives have between 16 and 128 MB of disk buffer. (To take drives that are currently on the market as an example, Western Digital's Black line of HDDs has either 32 or 64 MB of buffer, depending on the model.)

The function of this cache is primarily to sequence disk writes for optimum performance and manage and execute read requests from a client (such as the CPU or OS) in a strategic way.

Put another way, when we keep in mind that the bus attaching the physical HDD to the motherboard is rarely the same speed as the rotation of the hard disk platters and the mechanical motion of the read/write heads, the buffer stores data read from the disk before it's sent to the client; it likewise stores data to be written to the disk until the actual disk write can be executed. It's up to the buffer and the drive's processor to organize the data so it gets to its destination as efficiently as possible.

However accurate this explanation may be, it lacks concretion. *Linux System Administrator's Guide* offers a more concrete explanation (`http://www.tldp.org/LDP/sag/html/buffer-cache.html`):

> *Reading from a disk is very slow compared to accessing (real) memory. In addition, it is common to read the same part of a disk several times during relatively short periods of time. For example, one might first read an e-mail message, then read the letter into an editor when replying to it, then make the mail program read it again when copying it to a folder. Or, consider how often the command ls might be run on a system with many users. By reading the information from disk only once and then keeping it in memory until no longer needed, one can speed up all but the first read. This is called disk buffering, and the memory used for the purpose is called the buffer cache.*

We must choose from among five cache options to define a Proxmox VE VM: the default is **No Cache**. The following alternatives are available:

- Direct sync
- Write Through
- Write back
- Write back (unsafe)

There's a very clear, concise, general-purpose differentiation between write-through and write-back caches offered at `https://simple.wikipedia.org/wiki/Cache#Caches_for_writing`.

Write back is KVM-QEMU's default; note Proxmox VE's default is instead **No cache**.

While the resources are ordered from most to least pertinent, each provides a helpful perspective and is included precisely because, when we rely on all three, we can begin to start conceptualizing use cases for each mode. The following list provides resources that describe each of these modes.

- `https://access.redhat.com/documentation/en-US/Red_Hat_Enterprise_Linux/7/html/Virtualization_Tuning_and_Optimization_Guide/sect-Virtualization_Tuning_Optimization_Guide-BlockIO-Caching.html`: From *Virtualization Tuning and Optimization Guide* from Red Hat
- `https://www.suse.com/documentation/sles11/book_kvm/data/sect1_1_chapter_book_kvm.html`: From *Virtualization with KVM* and provided by SUSE
- `https://www-01.ibm.com/support/knowledgecenter/linuxonibm/liaat/liaatbpkvmguestcache.htm`: From *Linux on IBM Systems*

To evaluate performance, we need either consistent anecdotes or structured comparisons of the performances of each combination of cache mode, bus, and virtual disk format.

The most thorough and visually compelling results available on the Web are published at `http://jrs-s.net/2013/05/17/kvm-io-benchmarking/` (by Jim Salter, 2013) and `http://www.ilsistemista.net/index.php/virtualization/11-kvm-io-slowness-on-rhel-6.html` (by Ginatan Dante, 2011).

 Additional benchmarks, specific to Proxmox VE, are posted at `http://i51.tinypic.com/158bc14.gif`; however, the results are posted without offering methodology, version, date, or attribution info.

The benchmarks provided in these studies from 2011 and 2013 are a helpful starting point, but significantly conflict with the KVM best practice statements.

These investigations sometimes resonate, but can also conflict with Proxmox VE or the KVMs best I/O performance tips and testimonials available on the web.

- The investigations cited previously support virtio paravirtualizaiton as being the bus of choice whenever the choice is possible, which is anytime drivers are available for the guest OS.

- Generally, caching adds redundant data and bus traffic and ultimately will impact performance negatively. For best results, choose **No Cache** for RAW images and avoid the **Directsync** and **Write Through** cache options with QCOW2 images except when working with the ZSF filesystem and a RAID array as your primary storage.

- RAW is broadly acknowledged to provide the best performance among the three formats available in Proxmox VE; however, it's at the cost of the significant bundle of features QCOW2 images offer. The benefits of the feature set should certainly be weighed against RAW's performance, particularly with **No Cache** selected in combination with **VIRTIO**. If you rely on solid state storage, much of the performance difference between RAW and QCOW2 becomes unnoticeable.

- The Consensus from the Proxmox VE user community is that there is no practical benefit to building a VM in Proxmox VE with a VMDK disk image.

Proxmox VE and KVM-QEMU best practice resources
```
https://pve.proxmox.com/wiki/Performance_Tweaks
http://www.ilsistemista.net/index.php/virtualization/23-k
vm-storage-performance-and-cache-settings-on-red-hat-ente
rprise-linux-62.html?start=2
http://www.linux-kvm.org/page/Tuning_KVM
```

With the conclusion of this section, we have accomplished several objectives towards the goal articulated at the beginning of the chapter:

- We have the resources to make informed choices about appropriate bus/interfaces for our Proxmox VE VM guests
- We can now deliberately choose from among virtual disk image formats available for use through the Proxmox VE interface and can pursue further support as needed

Learning more

If this chapter sends any single message clearly, it should be this: optimizing the I/O performance of a VM in Proxmox VE involves carefully considering and combining three components, each with a very rich set of options—tuning a VM to perform optimally and with the features you want is a complex balancing act.

Consequently, a list of helpful resources is provided here so each of us can pursue more information based on our specific needs. The first two resources have rich chapters on virtual disks. The third is a work in progress that's thoroughly committed to virtual disk documentation:

- *Hands-On Virtual Computing*, Ted Simpson, Cengage
- *Virtualization from the Desktop to the Enterprise*, Chris Wolf, Apress

- *The Linux Sysadmins Guide to Virtual Disks: From the Basics to the Advanced*, Tim Bielawa, `http://lnx.cx/docs/vdg/output/Virtual-Disk-Operations.pdf`.

Summary

Our purpose in this chapter has been to understand virtual disks in the context of Proxmox VE virtual machine guests (the chapter does not address anything that concerns container guests).

We've accomplished a difficult task by focusing on how Proxmox VE, and its underlying virtualization technology, handle the abstractions of the components of physical hard disk drives: storage media, the bus interface, and the disk buffer.

As we proceeded, we worked hard to understand and be able to articulate how the choices we make when determining disk format, bus, and disk buffer preferences can significantly affect both features and I/O performance.

At the most fundamental level, we recognized that our VMs will not have better I/O proficiency than our physical host's hardware allows. However, you also learned that, by relying on paravirtualization drivers, you can minimize the overhead cost of virtualization on I/O performance.

To summarize, you learned that our decision making regarding virtual-disk configuration depends on how we answer some fundamental questions:

- What physical hardware do you already have that affects I/O performance?
- What are the performance needs of the application and/or database that the VM is dedicated to serving?
- What features of a virtual disk format should you take advantage of? Which redundant features can be provided by other technologies in your datacenter?

- What are the capacity needs of the OS and application and/or database?
- What are the administrators already familiar with and willing to support in terms of file systems, virtualization generally, and virtual disks in particular?
- What are the OS concerns and requirements in regards to file systems and bus drivers?

In the next chapter, we continue to build on what you learned in Chapter 4, *Creating a Virtual Machine*, about the creation of virtual machines by focusing on the Proxmox VE network model. To do this, we'll rely on our prior knowledge of TCP/IP LAN networks, switching, and subnets.

It'll be a great transitional chapter as we move toward understanding Proxmox VE and virtualization security.

Let's connect nodes and build bridges!

6
Networking with Proxmox VE

In Chapter 5, *Managing Virtual Disks*, we looked at one of the most flexible, and therefore complex components of virtualization: secondary storage. That flexibility and concomitant complexity is because we were attentive to performance and tuning I/O throughput to do the best we can in the face of the overhead implicit in this kind of virtualization.

This chapter gives the same attention to another opportunity to optimize I/O throughput: *the vNIC configuration of the virtual machine.*

Since vNIC optimization involves coordinating fewer moving parts, we're going to use this opportunity to address networking with Proxmox VE in a broader context—beyond just the optimization of the virtual machine, and to the design of networks that include Proxmox VE guests and hosts.

Throughout, we'll (strive to) maintain coherent focus on the Proxmox VE's networking model and the possibilities that model opens up for us. We'll cover the topic with enough detail to conjure up possibilities for enterprise network deployment. At the same time, we'll walk through configurations that make more sense in a small office context more consistent with our hardware.

We'll proceed as follows:

- Proxmox VE network model
- Configuring virtual machine guests

Proxmox VE network model

This section provides a high-level overview of the Proxmox VEnetwork model. It covers subjects relevant to both Proxmox VE guests as well as hosts.

In Proxmox VE 4.0, two fundamental guest network configurations are supported:

- Bridged
- Masquerading with NAT

The following subsection contrasts these two configuration models and establishes effective, sensible use cases for each.

The remainder of the subsection addresses Proxmox VE host configuration concerns:

- Routed configuration
- VLAN support
- NIC bonding

Bridged configuration

Bridged networking connects a Proxmox VE guest to a network using the host's Ethernet adapter.

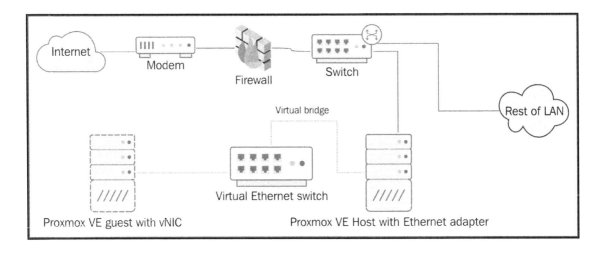

Visualizing bridged configuration

Virtual machines and containers with bridged connections behave precisely as if they're connected to the physical network. Indeed, each virtual server has a virtual NIC (or vNIC) that appears to the network with a discreet and unique MAC (media access control address) and IP address consistent with the physical network.

This is the default network configuration for Proxmox VE virtual servers.

As in the preceding illustration, it may be helpful to think of a bridged connection as analogous to attaching a physical machine to a simple network switch.

In *Mastering Proxmox*, two contrasting diagrams help illustrate how bridged networking works to provide an alternative to a more traditional infrastructure without virtualization. First, let's look at a traditional campus infrastructure:

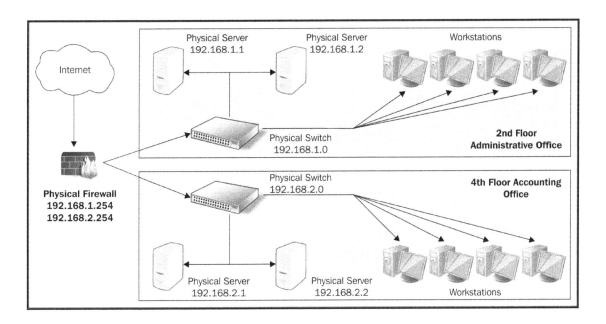

Visualizing a traditional campus infrastructure

The next diagram, also from *Mastering Proxmox*, represents a campus with a virtualized network infrastructure:

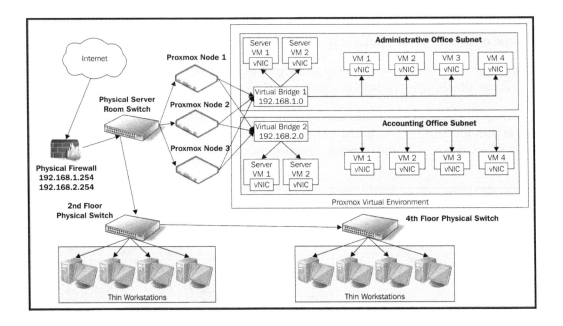

Visualizing the same campus with a Proxmox VE virtualized network infrastructure

NAT configuration

In some cases, you may want to hide a virtual server behind the PVE host's true IP address and masquerade traffic using **network address translation** (**NAT**).

In this scenario, the virtual machine or container has full access to network resources, but is not directly accessible from outside nodes. If a bridged connection is thought of as a kind of switch, NAT virtual servers may be thought of as being behind a router that partitions a public network from a private network.

With virtualization solutions and applications for workstations, such as Oracle's VirtualBox or VMware Workstation, NAT virtual machines make so much sense; they're fantastic for creating development and testing environments. They have full access to the LAN but, unless ports are forwarded, they cannot be accessed by the other nodes on the LAN. This is precisely what we want in the development and testing environments.

However, it may be hard at first to come up with a use case for virtual servers hosted by Proxmox VE, since the services wouldn't be available to users on the physical network.

Here's an example where NATing virtual servers is an ideal solution: several web servers are working together to provide optimal service availability. Each is listening on ports 80 and 443 (conventionally, HTTP and HTTPS respectively). For efficiency and efficacy, traffic is proxied through a load balancer.

As illustrated here, both bridging and NATing are used for the scenario described previously:

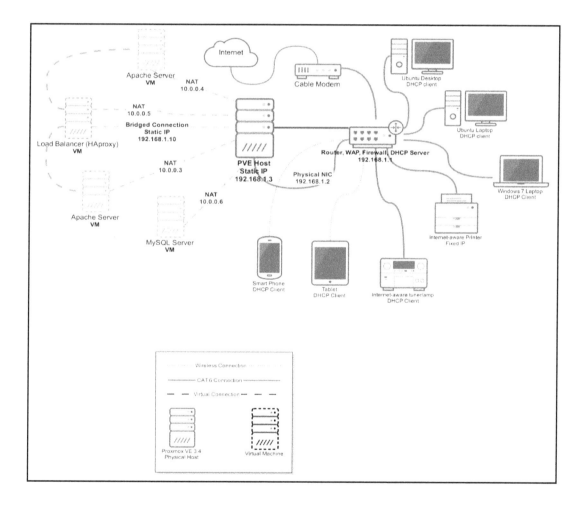

An example use case of using NAT and bridged configurations with virtual servers and Proxmox VE

Routed configuration

If your Proxmox VE instance is hosted by a cloud service, the bridged configuration described previously should not work. With an eye toward security, most hosting providers disable networking when they detect multiple MAC addresses on a single interface (`https://pve.proxmox.com/wiki/Network_Model`).

As a result, the bridged configuration provided here would likely not be functional:

```
auto lo
iface lo inet loopback
iface eth0 inet manual

auto vmbr0
iface vmbr0 inet static
        address 192.168.10.2
        netmask 255.255.255.0
        gateway 192.168.10.1
        bridge_ports eth0
        bridge_stp off
        bridge_fd 0
```

A common solution is having a single interface configured with a public, static IP (`192.168.10.2` for this example). Using a bridge, additional IP blocks are provided for the Proxmox VE guests (assume `10.10.10.1` with a subnet mask of `255.255.255.0` for this example).

The configuration for a routed solution scenario might look something like this:

```
auto lo
iface lo inet loopback

auto eth0
iface eth0 inet static
        address  192.168.10.2
        netmask  255.255.255.0
        gateway  192.168.10.1
        post-up echo 1 > /proc/sys/net/ipv4/conf/eth0/proxy_arp


auto vmbr0
iface vmbr0 inet static
        address  10.10.10.1
        netmask  255.255.255.0
        bridge_ports none
        bridge_stp off
        bridge_fd 0
```

The configurations offered are published on the Proxmox VE wiki page at `https://pve.p roxmox.com/wiki/Network_Model#Routed_Configuration`.

In addition, helpful information is incidentally provided in the Proxmox forum thread at `ht tp://forum.proxmox.com/threads/2034-Routed-setup`.

VLAN support

Proxmox VE supports VLANs in the network infrastructure.

A VLAN (or virtual LAN) is now understood as a group of network devices that are configured to communicate as if they were attached to the same physical network, when they are, in fact, located on any number of different LAN segments. In other words, on a campus where physical media intended for a single LAN are available, VLANs logically partition that monolithic physical network into a number of logical, or virtual LANs. Thus, based on logical connections rather than physical ones, VLANs provide an opportunity for enormous flexibility.

The procedure for joining a Proxmox VE host is outlined here; this process requires editing the text file at `/etc/network/interfaces`. Have the VLANs already set up in your infrastructure:

1. Create the bonded interfaces for each of the VLANs.
2. Edit your `bridge_ports` interfaces to match the VLANs you are using for management.
3. Rename your `vmbr` devices so that they reflect your VLAN.
4. After ensuring that the switch port that is plugged into the PVE machine is trunked using the dot1q encapsulation, restart the interface: `/etc/init.d/networking restart`.
5. Check your work using the `ifconfig` command.

The details are extremely contingent on the logical organization of the network; however, the Proxmox VE wiki has a guide with detailed examples at `https://pve.proxmox.com/wiki/Vlans`.

NIC bonding

Proxmox VE supports NIC bonding (or NIC teaming) out of the box, and it's configured very much as it would be on any Debian-based host.

NIC bonding is a strategy used primarily to increase fault tolerance on a PVE server. Bonded NICs that appear to have the same physical device have the same MAC address. Linux includes a kernel module called bonding to allow users to bond multiple network interfaces into a single channel.

> To learn more about NIC bonding with GNU/Linux and the pitfalls to avoid, please visit Charlie Schulting's article *Understanding NIC Bonding with Linux* at `http://www.enterprisenetworkingplanet.com/linux _unix/article.php/3850636/Understanding-NIC-Bonding-with-Linux.htm` (posted November 2, 2009). Linux Journal published another great resource called "Bond, Ethernet Bond" in 2011: `http://www.linux journal.com/article/10931`.
> To learn more about bonding with Debian, the GNU/Linux distribution upon which Proxmox VE is built, visit the Debian wiki at `https://wiki. debian.org/Bonding`.

The Proxmox VE wiki has an article on making the best use of bonding at `https://pve.pr oxmox.com/wiki/Bonding`.

The simplest resource for configuring a Proxmox VE host to take advantage of bonding is an official Proxmox tutorial on YouTube at `https://www.youtube.com/watch?v=-8Swp gaxFuk`. You'll find that, unlike VLAN configuration, bonding can be configured from the management interface alone; there's no immediate need to edit files from the command line.

Network configuration for virtual servers

Equipping a virtual machine or container with a vNIC can be a simple matter handled completely through the management interface during the initial configuration or subsequently as circumstances demand.

However, it can also be a fairly complex matter that requires modification of configuration files from the command line on the host, in the VM or container, or both.

In this section, we'll explore the simplest scenario: providing connectivity to VMs through the web-based management interface.

Providing basic connectivity

Here, we will focus on providing our virtual machines with basic connectivity and incorporate them into a flat network. We'll work first with VMs and then with containers.

Of VMs and vNICs

In Chapter 4, *Creating Virtual Machines*, we glossed over the configuration of the virtual network interface in the name of efficiency. Here, we'll discuss options provided by the VM creation wizard in the administrative interface.

Bridge configuration

First, let's configure a VM intended to be used with Debian 8 that's using a bridged connection. As previously described, a bridge configuration will integrate the VM into the LAN, making it fully available to other nodes, addressable with a unique IP, and identifiable by its MAC address. It's analogous to plugging a new physical machine into a network switch on the physical network.

Recall from Chapter 4, *Creating Virtual Machines*, that the **Create: Virtual Machine** dialog has eight tabs in total and that the **Network** tab is the seventh—the final tab before reviewing and committing your configuration for the new VM.

Here are the steps:

1. Download the Debian 8 netinst image and upload it to the Proxmox VE host using any of the methods described in Chapter 4, *Creating Virtual Machines*.
2. Access the Proxmox VE administrative interface at `https://<my-ip-addr>:8006` and create a new VM, specifying the netinst image in the CD/DVD tab of the **Create: Virtual Machine** wizard.

3. For this VM, the defaults on most tabs will be fine. On the **OS** tab, choose the **Linux 3.x/2.6 Kernel** option at the top right of the tab; on the **CPU** tab, ensure **Type** is set to **Default (kvm64)**. As discussed in the previous chapter, we'll choose **VIRTIO** as our **Bus/Device** on the **Hard Disk** tab with the **Cache** option set to **No cache**.

Configuring the hard disk

4. On the **Network** tab, we'll choose **Bridged mode** in the left column. The virtio paravirtualization driver increases performances not only for storage IO, but also for network IO. Since virtio drivers are incorporated into GNU/Linux, we're going to take advantage of this support by choosing virtio (paravirtualized) as the NIC model in the right column of the **Network** tab.

5. When you're all set, review your configuration on the **Confirm** tab and click on **Finish** to commit to the VM's creation.

6. Remember, you're not stuck with VNC options through the **Console** tab. Select the VM, select the **Hardware** tab, and double-click on **Display** to select **SPICE**.

Configuring the display for use with SPICE console option

Note that the **Hardware** tab also indicates that the configured vNIC for the VM has now been assigned a MAC. If you select **Network Device** and click on the **Edit** button, you should see a similar dialog to the one illustrated here:

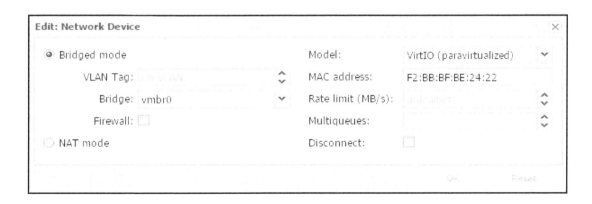

Configuring the Network Device

Now, get ready to start the installation, select the VM, click on **Start**, and drop the **Console** menu down to select **SPICE**.

At this point, follow the on-screen instructions to install Debian 8 to suit your taste. You'll have the option to use graphical installation — the screenshots shared in this section will be from that installation mode.

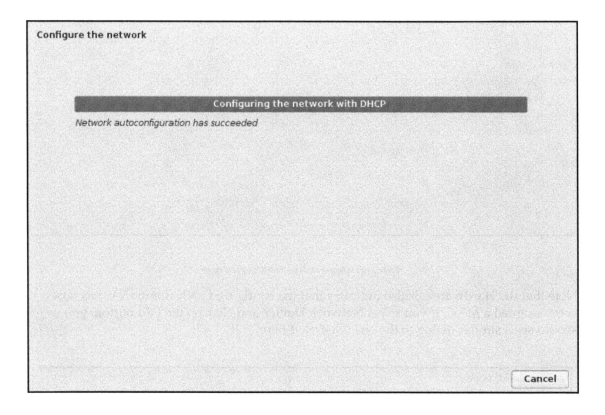

Networking works

At this stage, you have confirmation that your virtual machine has connectivity: if you glance at the management interface, you'll also see network activity:

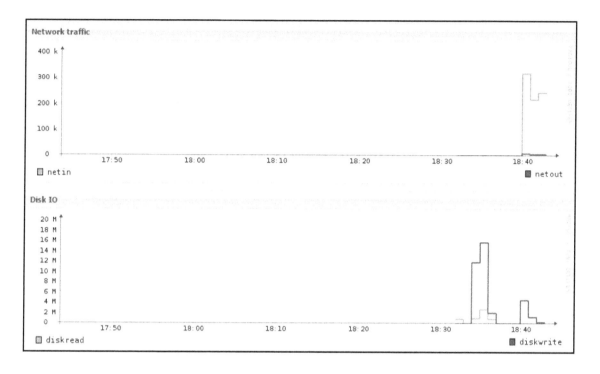

Network confirmed as working

Proceed through the installation until you are asked to specify packages to install. At that point, let's select just enough for a proof-of-concept of bridge configuration. Select **web server**, **SSH server**, and **standard system utilities**; click on **Continue** to complete the installation.

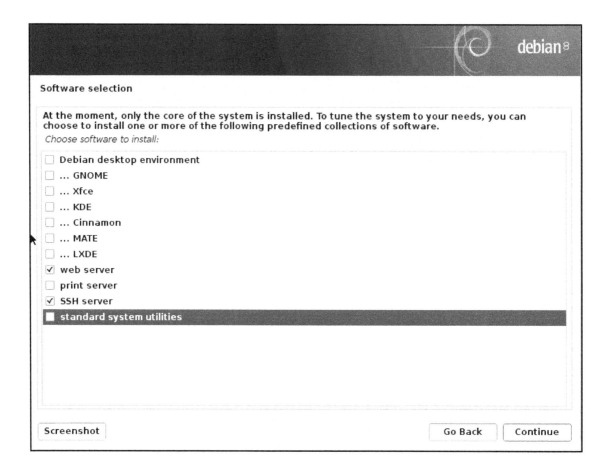

Selecting packages to install

With all the virtual pieces in place, when you click on **Continue**, you should be able to watch the progress as it downloads packages from the Internet and gives them a default installation and configuration:

Given a bridge configuration, when the installation is complete and the machine reboots, it'll be available at a dynamically assigned IP. You should be able to confirm this by accessing the machine via SSH or accessing Apache's default web page using your browser and pointing to port 80 on the machine.

On the other hand, nothing is confirmed without the IP address.

Unfortunately, the dynamically assigned IP isn't immediately available through the administration interface; we can find it through a scan, or we can simply use the console and ask in a terminal session.

```
root@debian8-temp:~# ifconfig
eth0      Link encap:Ethernet  HWaddr f2:bb:bf:be:24:22
          inet addr:192.168.1.50  Bcast:192.168.1.255  Mask:255.255.255.0
          inet6 addr: fe80::f0bb:bfff:febe:2422/64 Scope:Link
          UP BROADCAST RUNNING MULTICAST  MTU:1500  Metric:1
          RX packets:189803 errors:0 dropped:0 overruns:0 frame:0
          TX packets:484 errors:0 dropped:0 overruns:0 carrier:0
          collisions:0 txqueuelen:1000
          RX bytes:24037799 (22.9 MiB)  TX bytes:51618 (50.4 KiB)

lo        Link encap:Local Loopback
          inet addr:127.0.0.1  Mask:255.0.0.0
          inet6 addr: ::1/128 Scope:Host
          UP LOOPBACK RUNNING  MTU:65536  Metric:1
          RX packets:0 errors:0 dropped:0 overruns:0 frame:0
          TX packets:0 errors:0 dropped:0 overruns:0 carrier:0
          collisions:0 txqueuelen:0
          RX bytes:0 (0.0 B)  TX bytes:0 (0.0 B)
```

Using ifconfig to discover the dynamically assigned IP address of the guest

The preceding illustration shows the results of `ifconfig` in the new virtual machine: `inet addr`, the IPv4 address is 192.168.1.50. Users can now use any machine with a browser or SSH client to control the new web server, for example `ssh rik@192.168.1.50`, or `http://192.168.1.50` in this case:

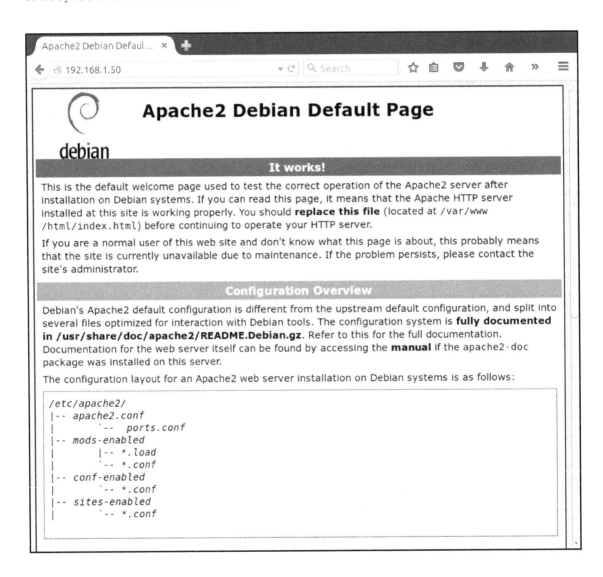

Successful Apache2 access from the LAN

We've successfully created a virtual web server available everywhere on our flat LANs.

As long as we keep using a dynamic IP, the address will not be reliable. Configuring a static IP address in a VM is not different from doing so on a physical machine. It depends on privileged access and knowing the routine and your network configuration; you'll need to have an available IP address in mind, and know your subnetwork mask, preferred DNS servers, and gateway. You'll also want your root credentials on hand.

Before you make changes, `/etc/network/interfaces` will look like this:

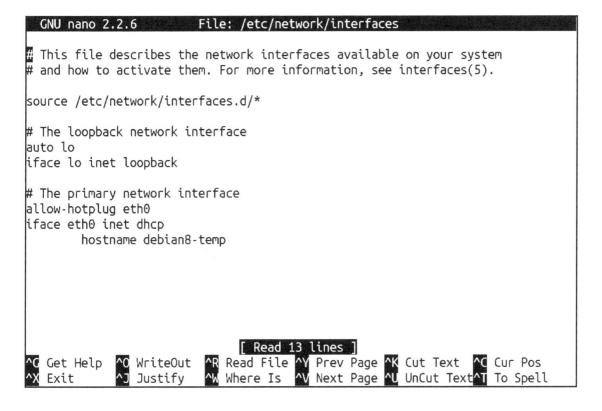

Interfaces configuration from the CLI

With my target configuration in mind, I can use `nano /etc/network/interfaces` to edit the configuration file to match it, as illustrated here:

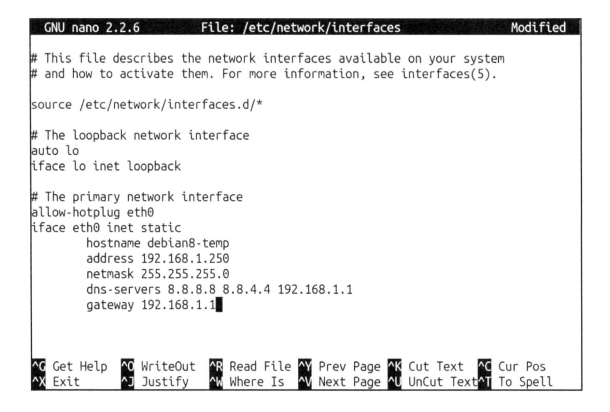

Editing /etc/network/interfaces in the guest

After writing out and rebooting, the web page should be available at the specified address, in this case `http://192.168.1.250`:

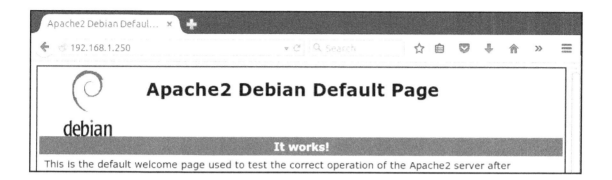

The Apache 2 default page

Use the `ifconfig` command to review the configuration of the network interfaces:

```
root@debian8-temp:~# ifconfig
eth0      Link encap:Ethernet  HWaddr f2:bb:bf:be:24:22
          inet addr:192.168.1.250  Bcast:192.168.1.255  Mask:255.255.255.0
          inet6 addr: fe80::f0bb:bfff:febe:2422/64 Scope:Link
          UP BROADCAST RUNNING MULTICAST  MTU:1500  Metric:1
          RX packets:656 errors:0 dropped:0 overruns:0 frame:0
          TX packets:189 errors:0 dropped:0 overruns:0 carrier:0
          collisions:0 txqueuelen:1000
          RX bytes:58888 (57.5 KiB)  TX bytes:20256 (19.7 KiB)

lo        Link encap:Local Loopback
          inet addr:127.0.0.1  Mask:255.0.0.0
          inet6 addr: ::1/128 Scope:Host
          UP LOOPBACK RUNNING  MTU:65536  Metric:1
          RX packets:0 errors:0 dropped:0 overruns:0 frame:0
          TX packets:0 errors:0 dropped:0 overruns:0 carrier:0
          collisions:0 txqueuelen:0
          RX bytes:0 (0.0 B)  TX bytes:0 (0.0 B)
```

In a home or small office setting, we simply forward a port on the WAN side to port 80 on the VM, and it will be accessible to the world.

In this subsection, we worked through an example of bridge configuration by creating a disposable Debian web and SSH server. We saw that using a bridge configuration, our virtual server is available to any node on the LAN, and potentially to the world.

In the following subsection, we'll quickly demonstrate NAT configuration with a pretty narrow use case.

Using NAT configuration

Let's adapt our Debian 8 guest. Instead of a virtual server, let's turn it into a desktop machine that's hidden from the rest of the LAN but accessible to users with access rights via PVE's web-administration console.

1. Log in to the administrative interface, select the Debian VM we created in the preceding subsection, shut it down, and select its **Hardware** tab.
2. Select the **Network Device** line and click on the **Delete** button to remove the interface.
3. Click on the **Add** button and select **Network device**, as illustrated here.
4. In the **Add: Network Device** dialog, select **NAT mode** in the left column and choose **VirtIO (paravirtualized)** from the **Model** drop-down menu.

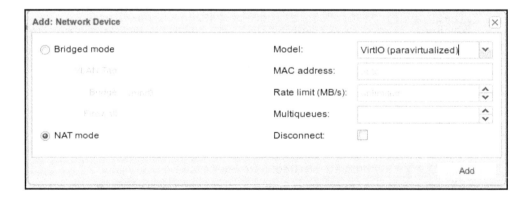

Setting up a network device with NAT configuration

5. Enter the VM with the console, and return the interface's configuration to its prior state by entering `nano /etc/network/interfaces` and editing the file as it appears here:

```
  GNU nano 2.2.6           File: /etc/network/interfaces

# This file describes the network interfaces available on your system
# and how to activate them. For more information, see interfaces(5).

source /etc/network/interfaces.d/*

# The loopback network interface
auto lo
iface lo inet loopback

# The primary network interface
allow-hotplug eth0
iface eth0 inet dhcp




                           [ Read 12 lines ]
^G Get Help   ^O WriteOut   ^R Read File  ^Y Prev Page  ^K Cut Text   ^C Cur Pos
^X Exit       ^J Justify    ^W Where Is   ^V Next Page  ^U UnCut Text ^T To Spell
```

Setting up a network device with NAT configuration

6. Restart networking with `/etc/init.d/networking restart`.
7. Confirm your new address by entering `ifconfig` to see results similar to those illustrated here:

```
root@deb8:~# ifconfig
eth0      Link encap:Ethernet  HWaddr 6a:b4:04:b9:ba:98
          inet addr:10.0.2.15  Bcast:10.0.2.255  Mask:255.255.255.0
          inet6 addr: fe80::68b4:4ff:feb9:ba98/64 Scope:Link
          UP BROADCAST RUNNING MULTICAST  MTU:1500  Metric:1
          RX packets:483274 errors:0 dropped:0 overruns:0 frame:0
          TX packets:253323 errors:0 dropped:0 overruns:0 carrier:0
          collisions:0 txqueuelen:1000
          RX bytes:723457245 (689.9 MiB)  TX bytes:13849963 (13.2 MiB)

lo        Link encap:Local Loopback
          inet addr:127.0.0.1  Mask:255.0.0.0
          inet6 addr: ::1/128 Scope:Host
          UP LOOPBACK RUNNING  MTU:65536  Metric:1
          RX packets:11 errors:0 dropped:0 overruns:0 frame:0
          TX packets:11 errors:0 dropped:0 overruns:0 carrier:0
          collisions:0 txqueuelen:0
          RX bytes:940 (940.0 B)  TX bytes:940 (940.0 B)
```

Results of ifconfig

At this point, the VM is accessible only to the Proxmox VE host and cunningly masqueraded behind its IP address.

Let's access it and configure the VM for virtual desktop access through **SPICE**.

1. Make sure the Debian 8 VM machine is selected.
2. Drop down the **Console** menu and select **SPICE**. You should be prompted to log in to a terminal session. Login with the root credentials.
3. At the prompt, enter `tasksel` and press *Enter* to launch the package configuration tool.
4. In the menu, select the **GNU/Linux Desktop** you'd like to try; in the following screenshot, **LXDE** is selected specifically because it is lightweight and our drive space is minimal.

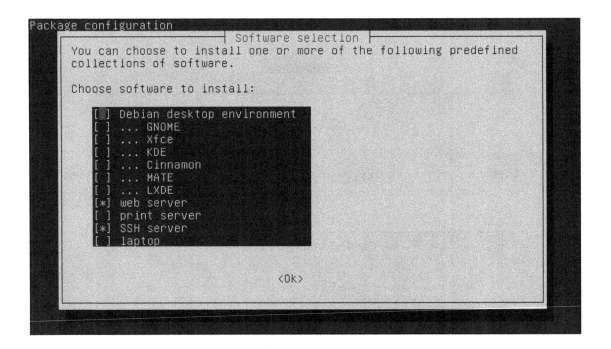

The package configuration before adding the desktop environment

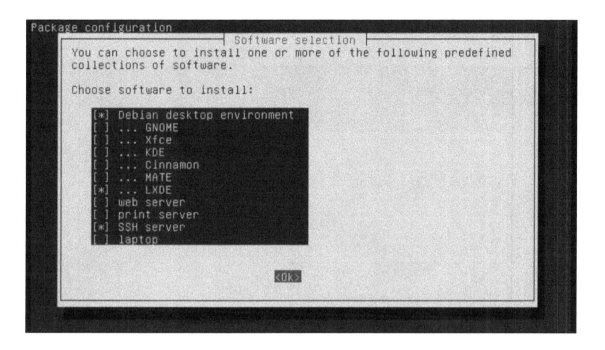

Package configuration
┌─────────────────────┤ Software selection ├─────────────────────┐
You can choose to install one or more of the following predefined
collections of software.

Choose software to install:

    [*] Debian desktop environment
    [ ] ... GNOME
    [ ] ... Xfce
    [ ] ... KDE
    [ ] ... Cinnamon
    [ ] ... MATE
    [*] ... LXDE
    [ ] web server
    [ ] print server
    [*] SSH server
    [ ] laptop

                    <Ok>

The package configuration after choosing LXDE desktop environment

5. After the package installation completes, restart the VM with `reboot`
   or `shutdown -r now`.

Welcome to the LXDE desktop environment; log in with the credentials you created for the
first user during the installation of Debian earlier in the chapter.

Going immediately to a browser, we can determine that we have access to services on the LAN as well as the Internet:

Accessing LAN from the VM with NAT configuration

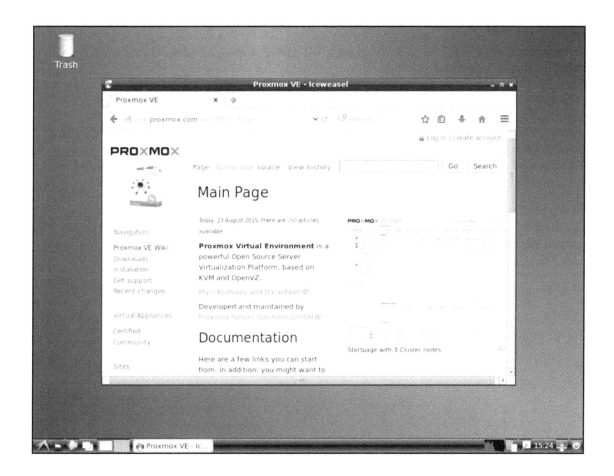

Accessing the Internet from a NAT-configured VM

However, returning to the physical workstation, we find that we have no access to the VM without going first through the Proxmox host.

Instead, we can access the new desktop through the console, and manage permissions with the feature-rich rights-management system Proxmox VE provides to restrict or permit access to VMs by specific users or groups (see `https://pve.proxmox.com/wiki/User_M anagement` to explore the rich rights management system in PVE).

Summary

We conclude having explored the Proxmox VE network model and worked through some configurations for virtual machines.

Along the way, our attention turned once more to virtio paravirtualization drivers—not for storage, as in the prior chapter, but rather for network IO. To briefly reiterate, virtio paravirtualization drivers for KVM-QEMU virtual machines help optimize efficiency by taking some of the sting out of the resource overhead associated with virtualization. Proxmox VE doesn't default to virtio, however; it defaults instead to the option with the greatest compatibility. In the case of vNICs, that default is Intel's E1000 NIC.

In the next chapter, we'll take a somewhat abstracted look at security threats and countermeasures specific to virtual machines, containers, and their hosts. We'll take our first look at the firewall features built in to the Proxmox VE administrative interfaces, and we'll work to realize some of the countermeasures proposed.

That being said, let's harden our Proxmox VE hosts and guests!

7
Securing Proxmox VE

"Abstraction may be discovered or produced, may be material or immaterial, but abstraction is what every hack produces and affirms….To hack is to produce or apply the abstract to information and the possibility of new worlds"

– A Hacker Manifesto, McKenzie Wark

"Putting it bluntly, virtualization is deception."

– Data Center Virtualization Essentials, Gustavo Alessandro Andrade Santana

"The enemy knows the system being used…"

– Shannon's Maxim

"Security through obscurity is not an answer."

– Information Security: Principles and Practices, Merkow and Breithaupt

"Containers have quickly become a popular cloud-optimization strategy for enterprises, however, what do we really know about the security implications?"

– Kowsik Guruswamy

The end goal of this chapter is to support you in mitigating threats to the security of your Proxmox VE infrastructure.

We start by enumerating and articulating the potential benefits of virtualization on infrastructure security.

However, these benefits must not be relied on unconditionally or discussed uncritically; we must qualify them here.

Moreover, we must expose the potential security risks virtualization can inject into the infrastructure.

Ultimately, this chapter commits to providing strategies for mitigating security threats to our Proxmox VE hosts and guests.

Security assurance is, of course, a sprawling field, and often includes not only threat mitigation, but also policy making, monitoring, incident response, and forensics. Our focus here is exclusively on mitigating vulnerabilities specific to Proxmox VE hosts.

Towards that end, then, the goals of security are defined here in accordance with tradition:

- Maintaining the *confidentiality* of a system
- Assuring its *integrity*
- Providing consistent *availability* of services

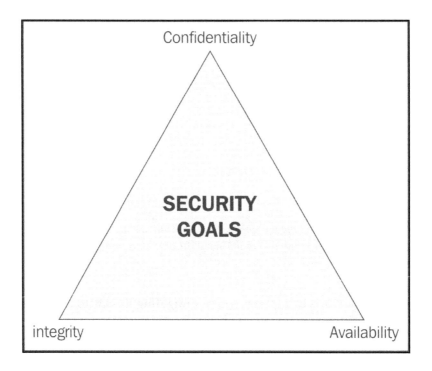

Security triad

The preceding illustration suggests that these three points are not isolated: the whole picture consists of three mutual relationships: one between confidentiality and integrity; one between confidentiality and availability; and, finally, one between integrity and availability. Too much or too little emphasis on one point distorts our Platonic triangle, a symbolic representation of our impossible ideal.

Given our end goal—mitigating threats—this chapter proceeds along the following vector:

- Examining the potential security rewards of virtualization
- Interrogating those rewards and exploring the potential vulnerabilities virtualization introduces
- Acting directly to mitigate threats

Security benefits of virtualization

Introducing well-planned, deliberate, and well-executed virtualization into an infrastructure delivers some very compelling security benefits.

"The abstraction of IT resources that masks the physical nature and boundaries of those resources..."

– Virtualization as defined by Gartner's IT Glossary (http://www.gartner.com/it-glossary/virtualization).

Let's be clear about one thing with regard to this common trope representing virtualization as a deceptive masquerade: security through obscurity does not work. The use of secrecy for the design or implementation of a system to provide security is a failing proposition. In enumerating the security benefits of virtualization, this section purposefully avoids suggesting that abstraction and the obfuscation it permits are an effective security strategy.

We'll see as the chapter develops that none of the security rewards promised by virtualization advocates can be realized without a good understanding of networking, systems administration, type 2 hypervisors, VMs, and containers. The following is also required:

- Rigorous planning based in part on defense in depth
- Flawless realization of those plans
- Excellent management throughout the lifecycle of all guests.

Given all of the preceding, there are very clear security benefits to virtualization with Proxmox VE:

- Reduction of the physical attack surface
- VM isolation
- Ability to restore to prior states
- Hardware abstraction
- Network segmentation support
- Encapsulation and portability
- Physical security
- Fine privilege control
- Integrated firewalls

Attack surface reduction

Moving to a virtual infrastructure reduces your physical attack surface in accordance with your virtual machine density. The more physical servers we convert to Proxmox VE guests, in conjunction with how densely we pack guests onto our Proxmox VE hosts, the fewer servers there are to ensure protection from potentially devastating physical attacks, for example.

Virtualization has an inherent potential to reduce the attack surface of an infrastructure in several ways; we'll focus here on how it reduces the number of physical hosts providing services.

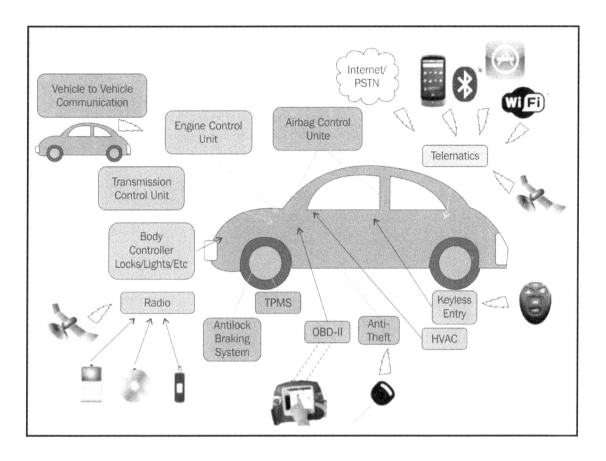

Visualizing attack vectors and the attack surface

Where we were once protecting, say, 15 machines from physical attack, there might be one or two physical Proxmox VE hosts to protect, for example.

We have to be critical here and realize this can open up new vulnerabilities and frustrating problems to resolve.

The Proxmox VE host becomes monolithic, so:

- If there's an unpatched vulnerability in Debian 8, PVE, or KVM and QEMU, the confidentiality, integrity, and availability of all the virtual machines hosted by that instance are also threatened.
- If an attacker gains physical access to the PVE host or hosts, the security and sanctity of all guests, both containers and virtual machines, are most certainly in doubt. If that's troubling, consider too that your snapshots and backups may have disappeared.

There's no doubt virtualization reduces the overall attack surface of your infrastructure, and in several ways; however, as articulated previously, this does not relieve us of any burdens, it just gives those burdens higher stakes while making them less complex to address.

Isolation

Virtualization encourages isolation. One VM doesn't naturally affect another VM, even if it is on the same host.

This tendency toward isolation suggests that destructive malware infecting a virtual server won't necessarily escape and spread to other virtual servers, even when they share a host.

If there's an oversight however, such as naively sharing data between two guests, or (worse) sharing data between a guest and the host, attacks can be devastating. Therefore, resist the temptation to create file shares among VMs on PVE; for the sake of security, do not share files between a Proxmox VE host and any of its guests.

Here the importance of documenting your infrastructure and writing a well-deliberated and well-enforced security policy is clear.

Availability of prior states

In the event an attack against a Proxmox VE guest succeeds, the guest can be rolled back to a prior state via backups or snapshots, effectively minimizing the time it takes to recover from an attack. (Note, however, that any data or information that changed between the time of the selected backup and the moment it is restored will be lost during a rollback.)

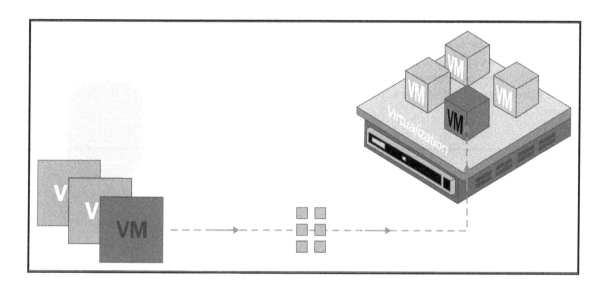

Rolling back involves applying a former version of a guest's storage file to the virtual machine or container

So, it's logical that the ability to restore to a prior state isn't an unconditional advantage of virtualization, even if it's an integrated feature of Proxmox VE; snapshots and backups must be integral to the well-thought out and executed lifecycle of the PVE guests and part of a well-defined and enforced policy.

Hardware abstraction

A fundamentally compelling characteristic of full virtualization is the abstraction of a computer from the physical hardware.

Imagine that a Proxmox VE guest with a well-organized trove of information collected over months is compromised and its hard drive destroyed in an attack that would have rendered physical storage unsalvageable—destruction of storage on a virtual disk does no damage to the physical storage that hosted it. When prior states are available to restore from, a snapshot or a backup can be restored onto the same hardware.

Without condition, damage dealt to virtual components has no effect on the physical host. This is an inherent reward for abstraction.

Segmentation

If an infrastructure is to be virtualized with Proxmox VE, take advantage of the network segmentation technologies it supports, such as VLAN tags, bridges, IPs masquerading with NAT, and per-guest firewalls. Use these technologies to make VMs or containers available to a limited population of users with legitimate business needs that call for a limited level of access.

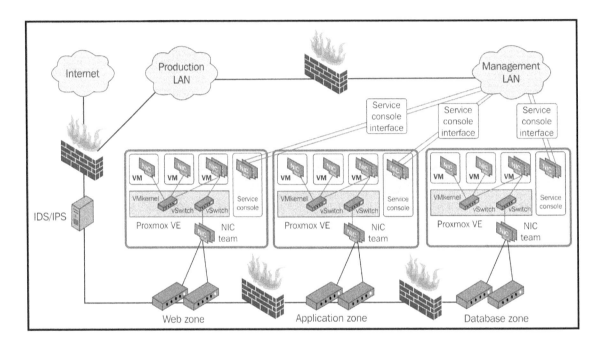

Visualizing segmentation and trust zones with Proxmox VE

To make the most of this valuable potential, think rigorously about sufficient trust zones as you plan your infrastructure.

 A trust zone is a network segment within which data flows relatively unrestricted, while data flowing in and out of the trust zone is subject to stronger restrictions.

 Open vSwitch
As an alternative to the bridges, bonds, and VLAN interfaces native to Linux, Proxmox VE supports Open vSwitch.
Open vSwitch is an open source, software implementation of a distributed, multilayer switch. It's production-ready and designed with virtualization specifically in mind.
To learn more about Open vSwitch, including features and potential drawbacks, visit its website at `http://openvswitch.org`. To learn more about Proxmox VE's support of Open vSwitch, visit the Proxmox wiki at `https://pve.proxmox.com/wiki/Open_vSwitch`.

Encapsulation and portability

As described in `Chapter 5`, *Working with Virtual Disks*, with full virtualization all information on virtual servers, including boot disks, is saved as a file; this is an example of encapsulation.

Invaluably, encapsulation serves the portability of the VM; even as an attacker works to compromise a PVE host, its guests can be moved, without halting, to another host in a cluster. Live migration—migrating an active guest from one PVE host to another in the same cluster—helps assure availability even in the case of an ongoing attack against a host.

 On Clustering and High Availability
For more on these topics, see *Mastering Proxmox, Proxmox High Availability*, and *Proxmox Cookbook* from Packt Publishing.

Physical security

When an attacker gains access to a physical server, the availability, confidentiality, and integrity it should demonstrate are absolutely in doubt.

To put it bluntly (and to appropriate a phrase from Scott Culp), if an attacker has physical access to your Proxmox VE host, it's not your host anymore.

As described previously, a very powerful benefit of virtualization is that the number of physical hosts decreases as the services they provided move to VMs or containers, effectively reducing the attack vectors, since the fewer machines there are to find physical space for, the fewer there are to gain illegitimate access to.

Nevertheless, include in your policy the procedures by which the PVE hosts, the storage, and the intermediate distribution frame (that is, the wiring closet) are to be physically secured against illegitimate access, and enforce the policy consistently and without exception; this means you've mitigated a potentially devastating threat.

Fine privilege control

With defense in depth and the principle of least-privilege in mind, consider the fine control of user access and restrictions that's realized when each service is moved to a discrete VM or container — in contrast to keeping multiple services running on a single physical server.

In a virtual infrastructure, a user privileged to access one service is not explicitly privileged to another as we can imagine they would be if the services were shared on a single hardware server. We can restrict access to Debian, finely define a user's role in relation to each VM and container via the PVE web interface, and further refine privileges on the guest OS level and the application level.

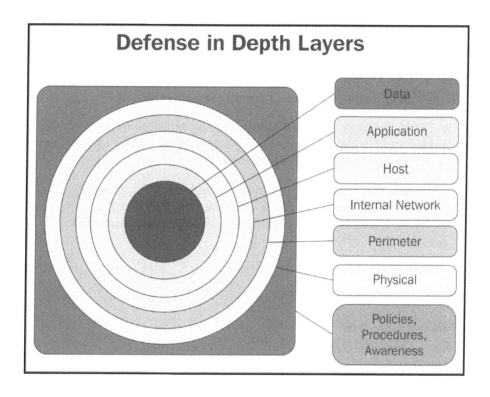

Some layers to consider in the practice of "defense in depth"

By default, the Proxmox VE management interface is authorized through GNU/Linux's default authentication system (**PAM**), and root is the only user. However, the authentication system for the web interface can be changed from PAM to PVE's system, to Active Directory, or to LDAP.

Whatever the authentication mechanism, specific users can be assigned different roles, or privileges, for each individual VM or container.

PVE User Management
To learn more about PVE's user management features, see the user management page of the Proxmox wiki: `https://pve.proxmox.com/wiki/User_Management`.

There are a host of predefined roles for users or groups that ship with PVE; and we can create new roles with different privileges and restrictions as necessary.

PVE firewall features

Proxmox VE provides flexible firewall features based on iptables.

These features can be configured via the administration interface or the command line to provide several layers of protection, as this allows rulesets to accept and reject traffic per guest server, per PVE host, and for an entire cluster.

To learn more about the Proxmox VE firewall, visit the official documentation at `https://pve.proxmox.com/wiki/Proxmox_VE_Firewall`, where detailed configuration examples are available.

It's rather critical that PVE be protected by a firewall.

Proxmox VE 3.4 relies on the following ports:

- 8006 (web interface)
- 85 (pvedaemon—configured to listen only on 127.0.0.1)
- 5900-5999 (VNC web console)
- 22 (sshd; used for cluster actions as well as a means to access a remote shell)
- 5404, 5405 UDP (CMAN multicast—if you run a cluster)

Proxmox VE 4.0 saw some changes to Proxmox VE's port usage:

- 8006 (web interface)
- 85 (pvedaemon-configured to listen only on 127.0.0.1)
- 5900-5999 (VNC web console)
- 3128 (SPICE console)
- 22 (SSH access-now optional)
- 111 (rpcbind)
- 5404, 5405 UDP (corosync multicast if you run a cluster)

Use your firewall experience to restrict access to these ports from subnets and IP ranges that don't have a legitimate need to access them.

Aggravated vulnerabilities

Virtualization's potential security benefits are certainly compelling, but many are quite conditional and altogether they are certainly no panacea.

Moreover, virtualization introduces new threats to an infrastructure—threats that otherwise either wouldn't be a concern at all or are exacerbated by virtualization.

This section calls attention to vulnerabilities that are historically problematic for virtual infrastructures:

- Denial of service attacks
- VM escape and hyper jumping
- Server sprawl
- Growing complexity

Denial of service attacks

Denial of service (DoS) attacks come in a wide variety of flavors. However, the immediate intent is the same: overwhelming a network, and its administrators, by generating large amounts of illegitimate traffic.

Distributed denial of service (DDoS) and DoS attacks are cheap, effective, and increasingly common. On the surface, they seem to be most effective at rendering services unavailable or unusable. More insidious, perhaps, is that, by keeping administrators' hands full as they cope with illegitimate traffic, other attacks can be launched without attracting their immediate attention.

Unfortunately, DoS attacks are particularly powerful against virtual infrastructures, wherein overwhelmed virtual hosts will certainly threaten the availability of virtual guests and the services they provide.

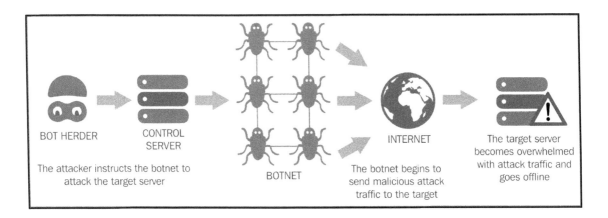

Visualizing a DDoS attack

In addition, research published in 2013 found that DoS attacks are significantly more potent where virtual machines are involved:

> *"[Under] DoS attack, the performance of a web server hosted in a VM can degrade by up to 23%, while that of a nonvirtualized server hosted on the same hardware degrades by only 8%. Even with relatively light attacks, the file system and memory access performance of hypervisor-based virtualization degrades at a much higher rate than their nonvirtualized counterparts."*
>
> *– Performance of Virtual Machines Under Networked Denial of Service Attacks: Experiments and Analysis*, Shea and Liu, http://www.cs.sfu.ca/~jcliu/Papers/Performance ofVirtualMachines.pdf

Clearly, in some areas, we may take solace in some security benefits of virtualization; however, DoS and DDoS attacks are one threat we cannot turn away from.

When migrating services from physical machines to Proxmox VE guests, work to define and deploy not only preventative measures, but also rapid response protocols. This calls for the implementation of monitoring and alert systems, as well as a firewall configuration that deliberately takes such attacks into consideration.

Each type of DoS attack has its own array of detection and mitigation strategies. To mitigate against SYN flooding attacks, for example, see section three of `http://tools.ietf.org/html/rfc4987`.

VM escape and hyper jumping

Virtual machine escape occurs when an attacker successfully "breaks out" of a virtual machine and interacts with the host operating system.

In a similar vein, **VM jumping**, or hyper jumping as it is sometimes referred to, is the process of gaining illegitimate access to a virtual machine via another virtual machine.

Presumably encapsulated and isolated environments, virtual machines run operating systems that shouldn't know that they are virtualized; there should be no way to break out of the virtual machine to interact directly with the parent hypervisor. For the same reasons, it should be impossible to illegitimately access a virtual machine through another virtual machine.

VM escape exploits are particularly devastating since the hypervisor controls the execution of all of the virtual machines and containers on the host. Consequently, an attacker that can gain access to the hypervisor can then win control over every guest running on the PVE host; since the hypervisor is between the physical hardware and the guest operating system, a successful VM escape will enable attackers to simply circumvent security controls implemented on the virtual machine.

VM escapes and hyper jumping should be an intellectual exercise, a fascinating theoretical problem. Unfortunately, that's simply not the case.

During the production of this book, for example, several VM escape vulnerabilities have emerged. Perhaps the vulnerability that captured the most attention was the one dubbed *VENOM* by researchers (`http://venom.crowdstrike.com/`):

> "VENOM, CVE-2015-3456, is a security vulnerability in the virtual floppy drive code used by many computer virtualization platforms. This vulnerability may allow an attacker to escape from the confines of an affected virtual machine (VM) guest and potentially obtain code-execution access to the host. Absent mitigation, this VM escape could open access to the host system and all other VMs running on that host, potentially giving adversaries significant elevated access to the host's local network and adjacent systems.

"Exploitation of the VENOM vulnerability can expose access to corporate intellectual property (IP), in addition to sensitive and personally identifiable information (PII), potentially impacting the thousands of organizations and millions of end users that rely on affected VMs for the allocation of shared computing resources, as well as connectivity, storage, security, and privacy."

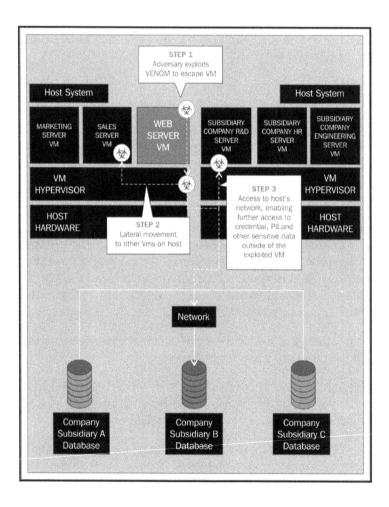

Venom attack scenario

Unfortunately, the many "computer virtualization platforms" invoked by the disclosure included all QEMU-based platforms; this includes Proxmox VE.

In the case of VENOM, a patch was available from Debian the same day the vulnerability was disclosed. A PVE administrator simply had to upgrade, in Debian fashion, and then restart guest virtual machines:

```
apt-get clean
apt-get update
```

After a shutdown and restart of all VMs on the Proxmox VE host, the vulnerability was gone. There was no need to even reboot the PVE host.

 The bug was introduced unknowingly in the QEMU source when the QEMU Floppy Drive Controller was introduced in 2004.

So it seems virtualization's celebrated isolation is not absolute.

From VENOM, we can learn some direct preventative actions that can be taken to mitigate emerging VM escape vulnerabilities:

- Keep Proxmox VE and Debian routinely patched. There are a variety of ways to automate the patching process; we'll walk through one method in the next section. Since Proxmox VE is patched through the same mechanism as Debian, patches to both are applied simultaneously.
- Patch operating systems and applications running on virtual machines and containers. On Debian and Ubuntu guests, use the apt tool; on Microsoft Windows and Server guests, set a reasonable Windows Update policy to ensure urgent updates are applied.
- *Don't* install virtual machine features you do not need. Doing so increases your attack surface unnecessarily. Be particularly attentive to what virtual devices are attached to your VM; if you don't need a virtual optical drive or floppy disk drive on the VM, either deliberately avoid installing them or remove them from the VM when you no longer need them.
- Avoid running software and services that are not essential to your guests' primary roles.
- However, weigh the benefits of running endpoint security software on a virtual machine; in his September 2015 article, "The Curious Case of the Escaping Virtual Machine," Bunmi Sowandi suggests that such software will detect malicious code trying to run in a VM before it has a chance to "escape". (`http://vmturbo.com/about-virtualization/the-curious-case-of-the-escaping-virtual-machine/`)

As we learned from VENOM, the best protection against VM escape and hyper jumping exploits is routine and well-thought out patch management.

Virtualization sprawl

In the context of virtual infrastructure, sprawl refers to the tendency of virtual servers to proliferate faster than administrators can properly manage. Sprawl encourages poor management decisions, hasty undeliberated action, sloppy configuration mistakes, and missed opportunities to mitigate threats.

From a security perspective, therefore, virtualization sprawl presents dire problems as administrators miss security patches, fail to harden services, and perhaps expose the network, the hypervisors, and storage nodes unnecessarily.

A helpful article on the Hewlett Packard site suggests some best practices to reduce the impact of sprawl effectively. Like many security issues explored in this chapter, the suggested solution is excellent planning, deliberated deployment, and writing and enforcing a security policy that includes VM lifecycle management. The article (`http://h30499.www3.hp.com/t5/Grounded-in-the-Cloud/5-ways-to-get-control-of-virtualization-sprawl/ba-p/6170959`) puts particular emphasis on the following:

- Whenever possible, create VMs and containers from "golden images" that include patches, patch policy, audit policies, software, and software policies

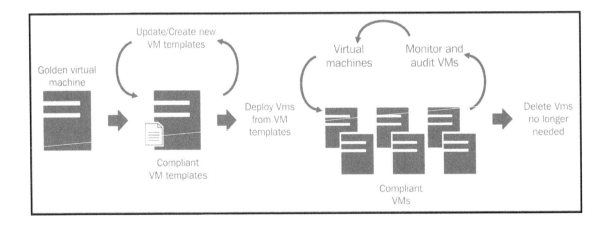

End-to-end lifecycle and policy management for VMs and VM template

- Proactively update policy-based enforcement on VMs as well as VM templates (and containers and container templates)

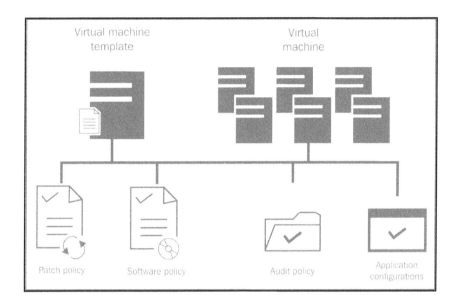

- Systematically manage the lifecycle and compliance of virtual servers from end to end (including, for example, routine snapshots or backups, and applying patches and upgrades)

The article is insistent on conveying two messages successfully:

- A well-thought-out security policy, which administrators can realistically comply with, is absolutely essential for keeping sprawl in check
- Tasks that can be automated must be automated

Virtualization sprawl encourages disorder; tame it with automation driven by a well-thought-out policy that's followed in the practice of daily administration.

At war with complexity

"A network architecture should be as clean and simple to understand as it can be. It should be possible to briefly…draw a few simple pictures to illustrate that design…."

"Having a clear understanding of the traffic flow on your network puts you in control of it. Not understanding the network puts you at the mercy of its vagaries."

– The Practice of System and Network Administration, 2E 2007

Given that virtualization encourages sprawl and given that secure virtual infrastructures demand segmentation, it's not entirely surprising that virtualization encourages problematic network complexity.

As network complexity goes up, so too does the pain that administrators suffer, since they must keep accurate documentation, troubleshoot connectivity problems on the fly, and sometimes provide actionable information for third-party support providers.

The "chaos approach" encouraged by infrastructure virtualization is not a reliable model to use in a network where the availability of every component matters (*The Practice of System and Network Administration*).

To limit network complexity, consider that the campus' network architects, engineers, and administrators should all be able to sketch, without aids, the key features and basic structure of the network topology.

According to Limoncelli, Hogan, and Chalup, the network architecture is neither clean enough, comprehensible enough, nor simple enough if this network map can't be relatively easily rendered. Maps of the physical and logical networks should absolutely be part of the system documentation and revised to reflect any modifications from the previous topology.

Taking the risk of sounding redundant squarely in the face, the best way to tame network complexity is to ensure the network can be explained and diagrammed, logically and physically, without the support of additional resources. If that's not the case, re-evaluate the architecture and see where it can be simplified without sacrificing security.

Taking action

If you're not yet virtualizing infrastructure, or you're not otherwise in a position to develop a strategic security policy, there're tactics you can take in the meantime to mitigate some threats to your Proxmox virtual environment:

- Secure the bootloader
- If possible, lock down the BIOS/UEFI
- Absolutely prohibit remote access to Proxmox VE's user interfaces
- Disable root access via SSH; consider prohibiting sudo access as well
- Use Fail2ban to prevent brute-force attacks
- Rely on key-based SSH authentication
- Maintain security patches for Proxmox VE and its guests
- Consider an enterprise support subscription

The practical procedures that follow are a strong (and immediate) complement to the less concrete strategies articulated previously.

This concluding section thus walks through these immediate tactical mitigation objectives to provide immediate support as you come to terms with Proxmox VE.

Protecting the boot process

In this section, we work to assure that OS and application-level authentication isn't rendered useless by an attacker with physical access who can thoroughly bypass these mechanisms.

We can think of booting as a four-stage process:

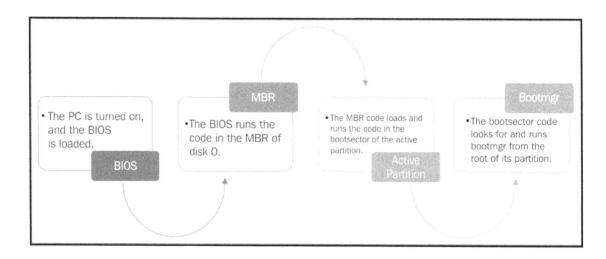

A generic boot process

During this process, the system can be vulnerable:

- An unsecured BIOS can be directed to boot from an attacker's storage device, allowing them to compromise the confidentiality and integrity of data stored on the Proxmox VE host and interfere with the availability of the services and virtual servers the host has intended to provide.
- By manipulating an unsecured bootloader, attackers can gain root access to a machine and compromise its confidentiality, integrity, and availability.

Using either method, the attacker effectively owns the machine. Let's do our best to lock down the BIOS/UEFI on our hosts and GRUB 2.0, the bootloader for Proxmox VE 3.4 and 4.1.

To learn more about the Debian bootstrap process, visit `https://www.de bian.org/doc/manuals/debian-reference/ch03.en.html#_an_ov erview_of_the_boot_strap_process`.

Locking down the bootloader

OS-level authentication restrictions can be very simply defeated on an otherwise secure Proxmox VE machine by manipulating GRUB 2, Proxmox VE's bootloader. See, for example, `http://linuxconfig.org/ubuntu-14-04-lost-password-recovery`, wherein the process is fully articulated. The gist of an attack looks like this:

1. Reboot and enter the GRUB 2 menu immediately after startup.
2. Modify the boot options.
3. Boot the system based on your modifications.
4. Change the root password of the system.
5. Shutdown and restart.
6. Login with the new password.

For an experienced GNU/Linux administrator, it's likely a familiar process; it's identical to how we reset a lost root password.

GRUB 2 offers extensive customization, and with it, the power to disable access to GRUB 2 options generally, as well as to specific menu options.

We will walk through the universal protection of GRUB 2 menu entries to enable access by a single superuser with an unencrypted password. This will prohibit attackers as well as sloppy or disgruntled colleagues from editing a GRUB entry or accessing a GRUB command line.

To follow this procedure, you must:

- Have root privileges
- Determine a superuser name and password to be used (we will use the name `admin` and the password `pve`)
- Edit GRUB configuration files from the command line
- Update the GRUB 2 configuration with the update-grub command

Let's get started:

1. Log into a shell on your Proxmox VE host; if PVE is configured with an IP address of 192.168.1.200, access a shell via SSH from a workstation on the same network:

   ```
   ssh root@192.168.1.200
   ```

2. Open `/etc/grub.d/00_header` using a plaintext editor; this example uses `nano` as the editor:

```
nano /etc/grub.d/00_header
```

3. Append the following lines to the bottom of the text:

```
cat << EOF
set superusers="admin"
password admin pve
EOF
```

4. Save the document and exit the editor; in `nano`, use *Ctrl +X*, then *Y*, and then *Enter* to return to a shell prompt.

5. Open `/etc/grub.d/10_linux` in `nano`:

```
nano /etc/grub.d/10_linux
```

6. Seek the following group of lines in `/etc/grub.d/10_linux`:

```
    echo "menuentry '$(echo "$title" | grub_quote)' ${CLASS}
\$menuentry_id_option 'gnulinux-$version-$type-$boot_device_id' {" | sed
"s/^/$submenu_indentation/"
else
    echo "menuentry '$(echo "$os" | grub_quote)' ${CLASS}
\$menuentry_id_option 'gnulinux-simple-$boot_device_id' {" | sed
"s/^/$submenu_indentation/"
```

7. In the last line, insert `--unrestricted` between `${CLASS}` and `\$menuentry`; the resultant line appears as follows:

```
    echo "menuentry '$(echo "$os" | grub_quote)' ${CLASS} --unrestricted
\$menuentry_id_option 'gnulinux-simple-$boot_device_id' {" | sed
"s/^/$submenu_indentation/"
```

8. Save the revised document and exit the editor; in `nano`, use *Ctrl + X* to exit, press *Y* to confirm, and then press *Enter* to return to a shell prompt.

9. Finally, prompt GRUB 2 to reconfigure itself based on the changes:

```
update-grub
```

When you reboot, you should find that PVE will start normally if left uninterrupted. However, if you try to edit a menu entry, boot from a submenu, or access a GRUB command line, you should find that you're required to authenticate.

For more on GRUB security, visit the following links:
`https://help.ubuntu.com/community/Grub2/Passwords`
`http://www.gnu.org/software/grub/manual/grub.html#Securit`
`y`

As the article at `http://opensourceforu.efytimes.com/2013/03/playing-hide-an`
`d-seek-with-passwords/` points out, this password can still be bypassed by configuring
BIOS/UEFI to boot from the attacker's boot device. If your hardware allows, you probably
want to secure this first stage of the boot process so would-be malefactors won't be able to
finagle the Proxmox VE host to boot from their own devices.

Locking down BIOS/UEFI

By securing the bootloader, GRUB 2, we can prevent a user from bypassing OS security and
gaining root privileges on the Proxmox VE host.

However, attackers can still simply bypass even the bootloader's security by booting instead
from their own media. From there, they can mount the machine's secondary storage and
make immediate decisions for you about its confidentiality and integrity. If an attacker is
particularly deliberate, he/she can install a cunning means to access the machine remotely
at a later date.

To mitigate this threat, we can, depending on our firmware, password protect the boot
device settings in either the BIOS or UEFI.

Since there's an unwieldy array of BIOS and UEFI firmware vendors, we'll articulate a
vision for what we'd like to do, and then hope our systems will cooperate.

The objective is to manipulate the BIOS/UEFI so it operates as follows:

- Allows the system to cold-boot without any interruption
- Requires authentication to change the boot device
- Prohibits entering the setup manager without authentication

This configuration can be tricky and is largely contingent on the BIOS/UEFI vendor.

Ideally, a machine with BIOS will allow you to do the following:

1. Enter the BIOS configuration when starting your PC. After power on, press the prompted key to enter **BIOS Setup Utility**; sometimes, it's the F key, *Delete*, or *ESC*. On some Lenovo machines, it's *Enter*. In the case of VMWare's PhoenixBIOS, *F2* is used to access the setup utility (access to this interface is what we want to make impossible or frustrating for an attacker):

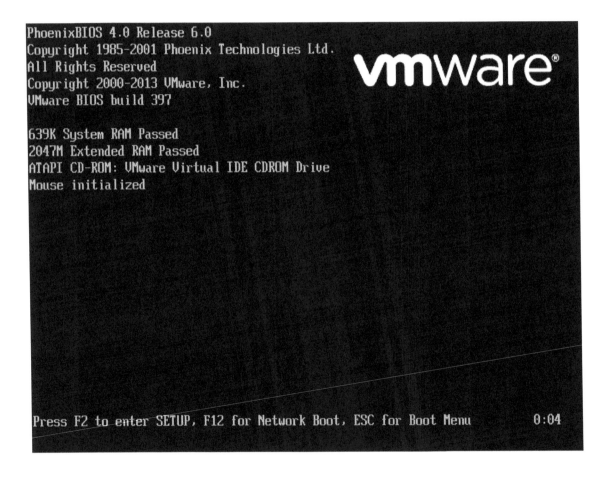

PhoenixBIOS, included with VMware Workstation, uses F2 to enter setup, F12 for network boot, and ESC for the boot menu.

2. Once you enter **SETUP**, navigate to a security tab. On the machines I've accessed, setting the administrator password will require the same credentials of anyone trying to enter the setup utility. On the PhoenixBios for VMware Workstation virtual machines, I can still boot without authenticating. So far so good.

3. However, when the preceding screenshot invites users to press *F12* for network boot or *Esc* for the boot menu, they'll find these are unrestricted. In this case, any attempt to lock down BIOS for security is really quite devastated.

4. If available, navigate to the boot settings in the SETUP utility. If the option is available in the Boot menu, disable devices that aren't used and that you don't want to use, such as network boot and boot from optical drives or USB devices.

5. Again, depending on availability, navigate to boot priority and set the boot priority of the remaining devices. Some systems allow you to use the *D* key to disable devices.

Ideally, your BIOS setup tool allows you to disable boot devices or password protect the boot device menu as well as the SETUP tool itself. Furthermore, it'll hopefully let you set a supervisor password without prompting you to authenticate to boot. If the boot process is interrupted to ask for authentication, there's the potential for a lot of unnecessary, and perhaps unplanned, down-time for the services users are relying on.

The settings recommended previously were possible in about half of the physical machines I surveyed for the chapter.

If your machine does provide for this ideal scenario, realize that, at best, losing the BIOS passwords means you've lost your license to reconfigure or troubleshoot the physical machine. In case of a lost password, you'll need to research how to bypass the security that you once felt was keeping bad guys out. The reset process is awkward, inconsistent, a time sink, and may not work.

It's essential, therefore, to keep a safe copy of any credentials you use to restrict access to BIOS or UEFI.

To learn more about securing the specific BIOS/UEFI system for your Proxmox VE host, look for the documentation from the computer or BIOS manufacturers or from community users on the Web.

If protecting the boot process to your satisfaction is not possible with the BIOS or UEFI you're stuck with, compensate by making sure access to the physical host is absolutely secure with alarmed door locks, key passes that log ingress and egress, and so on.

Secure Boot and Proxmox

Proxmox VE does not support the Secure Boot feature of UEFI.

Hardening the OS and hypervisor

The objective here is to ensure the security of both Proxmox VE (3.4 and 4.0) and Debian, its underlying operating system. Because Proxmox VE and Debian are inextricably bound, it's appropriate to address them together.

Prohibit remote access to the hypervisor

Pundits specifically committed to secure virtual infrastructures are insistent on this point: remote access to the hypervisor must be forbidden.

This directive must be qualified: it's absolutely appropriate it's absolutely appropriate to run a Proxmox VE host heedlessly (sans display) and to access it from another workstation on the same LAN via both SSH and the web-based administration interface.

What you want to avoid at all costs is making PVE ports, particularly 22 and 8006, public-facing and accessible to the Internet. Unless VPN is configured, Proxmox VE absolutely should not be available from outside the LAN.

 OpenVPN is an open-source package for providing VPN services; if you're considering a VPN solution, read more about OpenVPN at `https:///wik i.debian.org/OpenVPN`.

Harden SSH

Proxmox VE is designed to have two access alternatives:

- Access to a command line interface via SSH
- Access via the Web-based administrative interface

SSH must be an available option so administrators can make configuration changes to the underlying operating system. Moreover, as we saw in `Chapter 3`, *Creating Containers* and `Chapter 4`, *Creating Virtual Machines*, we may choose to take care of a significant amount of Proxmox VE administrative tasks via the command line.

So SSH can't be disabled outright in the name of security. However, in the name of security assurance, we must fine-tune the configuration of SSH to mitigate threats, whether from disgruntled or sloppy colleagues or outside attacks.

Our objectives here are as follows:

- Disabling direct root account access via SSH
- Mitigating brute-force password attacks against SSH
- Limiting access by IP
- Using encrypted keys rather than passwords to authenticate over SSH

Disabling root account access via SSH

This procedure is critical and absolutely necessary. First, let's create our own accounts with which to log in. We'll then use the new account to log in, escalate privileges using the `su -` command, and then follow a simple procedure to disable the root from logging in through SSH.

Once this procedure is complete, we'll log in using the new account for the foreseeable future; to perform a procedure that requires root's privileges, we'll simply use the `su -` command to temporarily escalate the privileges of this user account, by following these steps:

1. Choose a username and password you intend to use to administer Proxmox VE via SSH.
2. Via SSH, log in as the root using the credentials you created during the installation of Proxmox VE.
3. Use the adduser command, followed by the username you've chosen, to create a new account:

```
adduser rgoldman
```

4. Follow the prompts to create and confirm the new account's password.
5. Enter the full name you'd like associated with the new account.
6. You may choose to ignore the remaining prompts for additional information, such as office number, address, and telephone number.

7. Press *Y* and *Enter* to confirm the creation of the new user.

```
root@DevOps:~# adduser rgoldman
Adding user `rgoldman' ...
Adding new group `rgoldman' (1000) ...
Adding new user `rgoldman' (1000) with group `rgoldman' ...
Creating home directory `/home/rgoldman' ...
Copying files from `/etc/skel' ...
Enter new UNIX password:
Retype new UNIX password:
passwd: password updated successfully
Changing the user information for rgoldman
Enter the new value, or press ENTER for the default
        Full Name []: Rik Goldman
        Room Number []:
        Work Phone []:
        Home Phone []:
        Other []:
Is the information correct? [Y/n] y
root@DevOps:~# █
```

Creating a new user within a command line prompt

8. Use the `exit` command to close the SSH session.
9. Reconnect to Proxmox VE using the new account name:

    ssh rgoldman@192.168.1.200

10. Use the `su` – command to escalate privileges and enter the root's password to continue.
11. Edit /etc/ssh/sshd_config using nano:

    nano /etc/ssh/sshd_config

12. Seek the following section using the arrow keys or the *PageDown* key:

    #LoginGraceTime 2m
    #PermitRootLogin no
    #StrictModes yes
    #MaxAuthTries 6

13. In this file, the # symbol signifies that the line is a comment and is not to be considered as part of the SSH daemon's configuration. Let's remove the # symbol from the second line to enable the directive:

```
PermitRootLogin no
```

14. Save and exit the revised configuration file: *Ctrl + X, Y, Enter.*

15. We can restart the SSH daemon without it affecting our session:

```
/etc/init.d/ssh restart
```

15. Now, let's test to ensure root can no longer log in. Start by entering `exit` to leave the `su` mode, and `exit` again to close SSH.

16. Start a new SSH session as the root:

```
ssh root@192.168.1.200
```

Access should be denied, without the opportunity to enter a password.

Preventing brute-force attacks against SSH

As long as SSH daemon is configured to use password authentication, it's vulnerable to brute-force password attacks. One mitigation strategy is to install and configure Fail2ban, a powerful tool designed to detect attacks on a service and ban the offending IP address from which the attacks originate for a predefined period. Fail2ban effectively increases the cost in resources and the time attackers have to invest to continue a brute force password attack.

To make use of Fail2ban, follow this procedure:

1. Login via SSH and your new user account.
2. Escalate privileges:

```
su -
```

3. Install Fail2ban:

```
apt-get update && apt-get install -y fail2ban
```

4. Copy the default configuration called `jail.conf` to a new file called `jail.local`:

```
cp /etc/fail2ban/jail.conf /etc/fail2ban/jain.local
```

5. Open the new file in an editor such as nano:

```
nano /etc/fail2ban/jail.local
```

6. Cofirm Fail2ban's configuration for SSH in the following stanza:

```
[ssh]
enabled    = true
port       = ssh
filter     = sshd
logpath    = /var/log/auth.log
maxretry   = 6
```

7. Save the file and exit nano with *Ctrl + X, Y, Enter.*
8. If any changes were necessary, restart Fail2ban:

```
/etc/init.d/fail2ban restart
```

Fail2ban can also be configured to protect PVE's web-based administration interface from brute-force attacks.
First, add the following to /etc/fail2ban/jail.local:

```
[proxmox]
enabled = true
port     = 8006, https
filter   = proxmox
logpath = /var/log/daemon.log
maxretry = 3
bantime = 3600 # 1 hour
```

Then, create the filter by entering nano /etc/fail2ban/filter.d/proxmox.conf at the command line. Enter the following lines:

```
[Definition]
failregex = pvedaemon\[.*authentication
failure;
rhost= <host> user=.* msg=.* ignoreregex =
```

Save the file and exit nano with *Ctrl +X, Y, Enter.*
Restart Fail2ban to activate the new configuration:

```
/etc/init.d/fail2ban restart
```

With Fail2ban configured as described previously, failure to authenticate successfully three times in a row in the web interface will prohibit the client from connecting again for a full hour:

Unable to connect

Firefox can't establish a connection to the server at 172.16.118.128:8006.

- The site could be temporarily unavailable or too busy. Try again in a few moments.
- If you are unable to load any pages, check your computer's network connection.
- If your computer or network is protected by a firewall or proxy, make sure that Firefox is permitted to access the Web.

Try Again

After three unsuccessful attempts to log in to the PVE web interface

More on Fail2ban

To learn more about Fail2ban and how it works, visit `http://www.fail2ban.org/wiki/index.php/Main_Page`.

To learn more about Fail2ban and Proxmox VE, visit the Proxmox Wiki at `https://pve.proxmox.com/wiki/Fail2ban`.

Relying on key-based authentication

Another way to secure SSH access to a Proxmox VE server is to rely on key-based authentication instead of password authentication. The advantage to this authentication method is that you can disable password authentication altogether and not have to worry about the strength of legitimate users' passwords. Another benefit is that you can use the same key to authenticate to any number of SSH servers.

To make use of this feature, we'll start by generating an SSH key pair. Once you have a public and private key that can be used to authenticate, we'll place the public key on the PVE host so that we can use SSH key authentication to log in. Once these two procedures are complete, you'll check to see whether you can log in to your PVE host.

In the examples that follow, `rgoldman` is used as a placeholder for the username, while 192.168.1.200 is used as a placeholder for PVE's IP address. Please replace each as appropriate.

1. On a workstation on the same LAN as the PVE host, generate an SSH key pair:

   ```
   ssh-keygen
   ```

2. Confirm the key location at the first prompt by pressing *Enter*:

   ```
   Generating public/private rsa key pair.
   Enter file in which to save the key (/home/rgoldman/.ssh/id_rsa):
   ```

3. At the next prompts, you may choose to create and confirm an optional passphrase; using a passphrase will prevent an attacker from accessing the PVE host from your workstation. On the other hand, you'll have to enter the passphrase every time you wish to authenticate with the key:

   ```
   Created directory '/home/rgoldman/.ssh'.
   Enter passphrase (empty for no passphrase):
   Enter same passphrase again:
   ```

4. Look for confirmation that the key has been created — you should see an output to the terminal similar to the following:

```
Your identification has been saved in /home/rgoldman/.ssh/id_rsa.
Your public key has been saved in /home/rgoldman/.ssh/id_rsa.pub.
The key fingerprint is:
a9:49:2e:2a:5e:33:3e:a9:de:4e:77:11:58:b6:90:26 username@remote_host
The key's randomart image is:
+--[ RSA 2048]----+
|        ..o      |
|     E o= .      |
|     o. o        |
|          . .    |
|        ..S      |
|      o o.       |
|     =o.+.        |
|.  =++..         |
|o=++.            |
+-----------------+
```

An output similar to the preceding example confirms that you have a public and private key that you can use to authenticate.

Next, let's place the public key on the PVE host so that you can use the SSH key authentication to login.

5. Confirm the presence of the keys by listing the contents of ~/.ssh/; ensure that both id_rsa and id_rsa.pub are present in the results:

```
ls ~/.ssh/
```

6. Next, push the new public key to the PVE host using the ssh-copy-id tool with the following syntax (assuming the username is rgoldman and the PVE host is at 192.168.1.200):

```
ssh-copy-id rgoldman@192.168.1.200
```

7. That's it. Now confirm you can login without a password:

```
ssh rgoldman@192.168.1.200
```

If you were able to login to your PVE account using SSH without a password, you have successfully configured SSH key-based authentication for your account.

The image that follows illustrates the transaction:

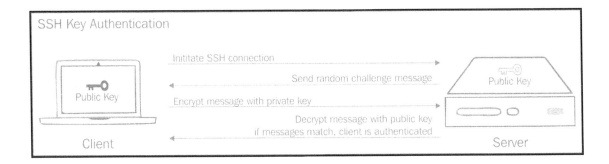

SSH key authentication

Note, however, that your password-based authentication mechanism is still active; the SSH server is still exposed to brute-force or social engineering attacks.

The following steps will disable password-based authentication on your server. Certainly, don't proceed here if you plan to access PVE from other hosts but haven't copied the key yet (or if you are not yet confident with key-based authentication):

1. Using SSH, log in to the PVE host from a local workstation.
2. Escalate privileges:

   ```
   su -
   ```

3. Open the SSH daemon configuration using nano or another plaintext editor:

   ```
   nano /etc/ssh/sshd_config
   ```

4. Browse the contents of the file for the following directive:

   ```
   PasswordAuthentication yes
   ```

5. Change the directive so it is as follows:

   ```
   PasswordAuthentication no
   ```

6. Save the file and close the editor with *Ctrl + X, Y, Enter*.
7. Restart the SSH daemon:

   ```
   /etc/init.d/ssh restart
   ```

We can now access Proxmox VE via SSH without worrying about the strength of our passwords or being vulnerable to brute force attacks or social engineering attacks.

Note, however, it's imperative when we rely on key-based authentication that we keep our keys absolutely secure. This means, in part, remembering consistently to lock our workstations and protect our workstation accounts with strong passwords.

Learn more about SSH
To learn more about SSH and authentication, consider visiting the following resources:
`https://www.debian-administration.org/article/530/SSH_wit`
`h_authentication_key_instead_of_password`
`https://www.digitalocean.com/community/tutorials/how-to-c`
`onfigure-ssh-key-based-authentication-on-a-linux-server`
`https://debian-handbook.info/browse/stable/sect.remote-lo`
`gin.html`
For additional hardening strategies for SSH, visit `http://howto.biapy.`
`com/en/debian-gnu-linux/system/security/harden-the-ssh-ac`
`cess-security-on-debian`.

Managing patches

As we discovered, the patch for the VENOM exploit was available for Debian the same day the exploit was made public; PVE administrators simply had to update and upgrade and restart PVE guests to eliminate the threat. This should drive home the importance of applying security patches not only for the Proxmox VE host, but also for its guests, whether they are containers or virtual machines.

However, routinely applying patches for several machines is tedious no matter the assurance it provides.

For the PVE hosts and Ubuntu or Debian guests, there are several tools to relieve the tedium. Finding the sweet spot between fully automated upgrades with minimal interactivity and doing due diligence to ensure patch candidates won't disrupt operations is where the magic happens.

In this section, we'll configure a tool called **unattended-upgrades** to routinely apply only security upgrades. We'll leave other patches to our best judgement.

Use the APT tool to install unattended-upgrades:

```
su -
apt-get update
apt-get install -y unattended-upgrades
```

Then, configure the automated security upgrades:

1. The default configuration file for the unattended-upgrades package is at `/etc/apt/apt.conf.d/50unattended-upgrades`; let's take a look at it:

   ```
   nano /etc/apt/apt.conf.d/50unattended-upgrades
   ```

2. Look for the following stanza (the `//` characters preceding some lines effectively comment out directives so they are ignored):

   ```
   // Automatically upgrade packages from these (origin:archive) pairs
   Unattended-Upgrade::Allowed-Origins {
           "${distro_id}:${distro_codename}-security";
   //      "${distro_id}:${distro_codename}-updates";
   //      "${distro_id}:${distro_codename}-proposed";
   //      "${distro_id}:${distro_codename}-backports";
   };
   ```

3. Ensure that the line with "`${distro_id}:${distro_codename}-security`"; is not commented out. This directive signals the utility to allow unattended-upgrades from security repositories, and only from security repositories.

4. Exit the configuration file by pressing *Ctrl* + *X*, *Y*, and *Enter* to preserve any changes you may have made.

5. Next, let's check the configuration of `/etc/apt/apt.conf.d/20auto-upgrade` to ensure that Debian is configured to periodically update package lists and that unattended-upgrades are enabled:

   ```
   nano /etc/apt/apt.conf.d/20auto-upgrade
   ```

6. Ensure that the following lines appear in the file as they do here:

   ```
   APT::Periodic::Update-Package-Lists "1";
   APT::Periodic::Unattended-Upgrade "1";
   ```

7. With unattended-upgrades configured, de-escalate privileges by entering `exit` in the terminal.

Changes made by the unattended-upgrades utility are logged in
`/var/log/unattended-upgrades/unattended-upgrades.log`.

The same package can be used to automate security patch applications for Proxmox VE guests running Ubuntu, Debian, or LinuxMint.

To learn more about the unattended-upgrades package, see the following documentation:
`https://wiki.debian.org/UnattendedUpgrades`
`https://debian-handbook.info/browse/stable/sect.regular-upgrades.html`

Enterprise subscriptions

Though PVE may be open source, Proxmox Server Solutions (the company behind Proxmox VE) very strongly encourages users to invest in subscriptions for Proxmox VE (`https://www.proxmox.com/en/proxmox-ve/support`):

"A Proxmox VE subscription is the easy and affordable solution to get access to the Proxmox VE Enterprise repository, to stable software updates and security enhancements, as well as to technical support services. A subscription helps you to run Proxmox VE with confidence in your company."

"By combining great open source software with quality-assured services and support the Proxmox VE Subscription helps you to deploy and maintain the best stable and secure open source virtualization environment"

Security wise, there is a strong advantage to obtaining a subscription: Proxmox Server Solutions provides subscribers with access to the enterprise repository, which provides stable and "enhanced" security updates.

In contrast, users of the `pve-no-subscription` repositories have access to patches that are perhaps more cutting-edge, but also less stable.

Another benefit of a Proxmox subscription is access to dedicated, professional support. This is far from a commentary on community support, which has in all cases been fantastic in my experience. However, subscription support will track a ticket and promise prompt solutions. In a production environment, this can certainly make a critical difference.

There are four subscription plans available: premium, standard, basic, and community (this last plan does not offer a support plan, but it does offer access to the enterprise repository). Plans are priced per month per CPU socket (`https://www.proxmox.com/en/proxmox-ve/pricing`).

> *"Subscriptions are licensed per physical server and CPU socket. In a Proxmox VE Cluster, you need to have the same subscription level for all your servers. Subscription period is one year from purchase date."*

Technical support is provided to subscribers via a web and email-based customer portal (in English or German).

Community support, by contrast, is available via the public support forum (`https://forum.proxmox.com`) or via IRC (the `##proxmox` channel on the Freenode network).

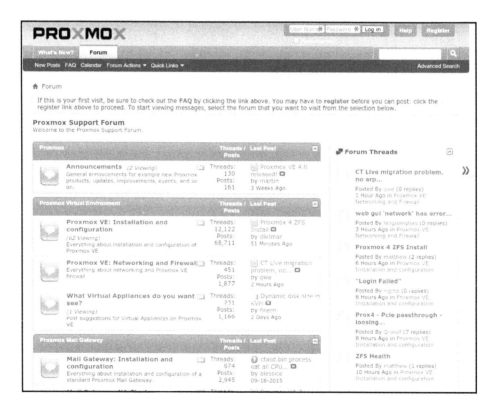

Proxmox community support forum

A video tutorial is available to guide subscribers in uploading a subscription key to Proxmox VE and installing new updates at `https://www.proxmox.com/en/training/video-tutorials/item/install-updates`.

From a security perspective then, the `pve-no-subscription` repository is characterized on the site as offering patches that are not quite stable enough for production, while the enterprise repository promises enhanced security patches. You'll have to make a deliberate choice for your use case.

If you're moving services that are not mission-critical to a virtual infrastructure with Proxmox VE, perhaps community support and the `pve-no-subscription` options will work well for you. Otherwise, give all due consideration to an appropriate subscription option.

Summary

The security and information that assurance administrators can realistically provide is clearly never as exhaustive as it is exhausting.

In the first section of this chapter, you learned that hardware virtualization has inherent security benefits.

However, you also learned that many promising benefits are undermined if they're not supported by thorough planning of the virtual infrastructure, explicit policy-making up front, and a flawless deployment, all followed by unflagging policy enforcement and ongoing virtual server lifecycle management.

We then outlined threats that are either unique to virtualized infrastructures or aggravated in the context of virtualization. Each point was followed by either concrete action to mitigate the threat or links to resources for more details on addressing a potential problem.

We concluded with concrete, step-by-step remedies that could be initiated immediately, even as you continue to explore and assess Proxmox VE.

Index

reference links 41
security 45
starting 68
stopping 68
suspending 69
copy on write 123

D

Debian bootstrap process
    reference link 184
Debian wiki
    reference link 27
Debian-based GNU/Linux distributions 10
default network configuration 139
Dell Poweredge R430
    reference link 22
denial of service 175
disk buffer 130
disk cache options 118
disk image formats
    QCOW2 119
    RAW 119
    VMDK 119
distributed denial of service (DDoS) 175
Docker
    about 76
dual-or quad socket server
    reference link 21

E

Elgg
    reference link 46
end-user license agreement (EULA) 30
enterprise subscriptions
    reference link 201
escape
    reference link 179

F

Fail2ban
    reference link 196
Fedora 23 Networking Guide
    reference link 113
Fedora 23 Server

features, reference link 114
installation link 103, 114
virtual machine, creating for 103, 107

G

GitLab
    reference link 47
GNU Social
    reference link 46
GRUB security
    reference link 187

H

Hard Disk 121
hard disk drives (HDDs)
    about 118
hardware virtualization extensions
    enabling 26
    installations, ensuring 25
hyper jumping 177
hypervisor features, Proxmox VE
    KVM 7
    LXC 7
hypervisor
    about 11, 76
    hardening 190
    remote access, prohibiting 190

I

IDE/PATA
    reference link 127
image formats
    reference link 122
integrated firewall feature
    reference link 96
Intel
    reference link 13
IPv6 64
ISO file
    uploading, to local storage 78, 79
ISO image, from remote workstation
    working with 78, 79